INFORMATION SECURITY POLICIES, PROCEDURES, AND STANDARDS

A Practitioner's Reference

OTHER INFORMATION SECURITY BOOKS FROM AUERBACH

Android Malware and Analysis
Ken Dunham, Shane Hartman, Manu Quintans,
Jose Andre Morales, and Tim Strazzere
ISBN 978-1-4822-5219-4

**Business Continuity Planning:
A Project Management Approach**
Ralph L. Kliem
ISBN 978-1-4822-5178-4

**Case Studies in Secure Computing:
Achievements and Trends**
Edited by Biju Issac and Nauman Israr
ISBN 978-1-4822-0706-4

**The Cognitive Early Warning Predictive
System Using the Smart Vaccine:
The New Digital Immunity Paradigm
for Smart Cities**
Rocky Termanini
ISBN 978-1-4987-2651-1

**Conducting Network Penetration and
Espionage in a Global Environment**
Bruce Middleton
ISBN 978-1-4822-0647-0

Data Privacy for the Smart Grid
Rebecca Herold and Christine Hertzog
ISBN 978-1-4665-7337-6

**Ethical Hacking and Penetration
Testing Guide**
Rafay Baloch
ISBN 978-1-4822-3161-8

**The Frugal CISO: Using Innovation and
Smart Approaches to Maximize Your
Security Posture**
Kerry Ann Anderson
ISBN 978-1-4822-2007-0

**Global Information Warfare:
The New Digital Battlefield,
Second Edition**
Andrew Jones and Gerald L. Kovacich
ISBN 978-1-4987-0325-3

**Honeypots and Routers:
Collecting Internet Attacks**
Mohssen Mohammed and Habib-ur Rehman
ISBN 978-1-4987-0219-5

Leading the Internal Audit Function
Lynn Fountain
ISBN 978-1-4987-3042-6

**Managing Risk and Security in
Outsourcing IT Services: Onshore,
Offshore and the Cloud**
Frank Siepmann
ISBN 978-1-4398-7909-2

**Multilevel Modeling of Secure Systems
in QoP-ML**
Bogdan Ksiezopolski
ISBN 978-1-4822-0255-7

PCI Compliance: The Definitive Guide
Abhay Bhargav
ISBN 978-1-4398-8740-0

**The Practical Guide to HIPAA Privacy and
Security Compliance, Second Edition**
Rebecca Herold and Kevin Beaver
ISBN 978-1-4398-5558-4

**Securing an IT Organization through
Governance, Risk Management,
and Audit**
Ken E. Sigler and James L. Rainey, III
ISBN 978-1-4987-3731-9

**Securing Systems: Applied Security
Architecture and Threat Models**
Brook S. Schoenfield
ISBN 978-1-4822-3397-1

**Security without Obscurity:
A Guide to Confidentiality, Authentication,
and Integrity**
J.J. Stapleton
ISBN 978-1-4665-9214-8

**The State of the Art in Intrusion
Prevention and Detection**
Edited by Al-Sakib Khan Pathan
ISBN 978-1-4822-0351-6

Web Security: A WhiteHat Perspective
Hanqing Wu and Liz Zhao
ISBN 978-1-4665-9261-2

AUERBACH PUBLICATIONS
www.auerbach-publications.com • To Order Call: 1-800-272-7737 • E-mail: orders@crcpress.com

INFORMATION SECURITY POLICIES, PROCEDURES, AND STANDARDS

A Practitioner's Reference

DOUGLAS J. LANDOLL

CRC Press
Taylor & Francis Group
Boca Raton London New York

CRC Press is an imprint of the
Taylor & Francis Group, an **Informa** business

AN AUERBACH BOOK

CRC Press
Taylor & Francis Group
6000 Broken Sound Parkway NW, Suite 300
Boca Raton, FL 33487-2742

© 2016 by Taylor & Francis Group, LLC
CRC Press is an imprint of Taylor & Francis Group, an Informa business

No claim to original U.S. Government works

Printed on acid-free paper
Version Date: 20160401

International Standard Book Number-13: 978-1-4822-4589-9 (Hardback)

Library of Congress Cataloging-in-Publication Data

Names: Landoll, Douglas J., author.
Title: Information security policies, procedures, and standards : a
practitioner's reference / Douglas J. Landoll.
Description: Boca Raton, FL : CRC Press, 2016. | Includes bibliographical
references and index.
Identifiers: LCCN 2015040188 | ISBN 9781482245899 (alk. paper)
Subjects: LCSH: Business--Data processing--Security measures. | Data
protection. | Computer security.
Classification: LCC HF5548.37 .L3577 2016 | DDC 658.4/78--dc23
LC record available at https://lccn.loc.gov/2015040188

Visit the Taylor & Francis Web site at
http://www.taylorandfrancis.com

and the CRC Press Web site at
http://www.crcpress.com

To All Those Who Inspire Me to Write: Here's to transformations. Thanks for helping me to turn the ideas for this book into words and more importantly for helping me turn happiness to joy.

To All Those Who Pick Up This Book: This book represents the transformation of thoughts put into words. It is up to you to put these words into action.

Contents

Preface

In 2006, I published my first book for the information security professional. There was a clear need for a book written at the level of the information security engineer who required a guide on exactly how to perform an information security risk assessment. At the time (and still today), no other book was available that illustrated the steps required to execute an effective assessment of an organization's information security controls. Now, in its second edition, *The Security Risk Assessment Handbook* continues to provide directions, techniques, and time-tested methods to properly perform one of the most difficult tasks in information security governance.

Since the publishing of the *Handbook*, I have performed hundreds of information security risk assessments and have prioritized existing security risks within retail, government, and financial organizations. These risks have covered all the corners of technical, physical, and administrative controls but by far, the most prevalent and misunderstood information security risks have centered around the organization's security policies. Most organizations lack a complete set of information security policies. Those organizations that do have policies have either antiquated documents effectively no longer in use or have cut and pasted their names into a cobbled set of disparate policies downloaded from various sources. In most cases, the organization is without any method to convey management intent on how organizational resources are to be handled or minimum-security controls are to be in place.

For the information security professional attempting to write information security policies, there has been a near absence of useful guides about the creative process. Sure, there are several good references of preexisting policies but this only further encourages the cut-and-paste approach and creates policies that do not fit the culture and operations of the organization. I wrote this book for the same reason as I wrote the *Handbook*. Information security professionals lack a guide to the creation (or revision) of an information security policy set. I have attempted to include policy-writing tips and tricks, techniques, and time-tested methods that I have used over the past several decades of creating policies for organizations. I encourage the reader to utilize these techniques and approaches but to remember that each organization is unique in its mission, technology, culture, and industry and to strive to create policies that truly match the intent of senior management and properly direct the appropriate use of technology and adequate information security controls.

Author

Douglas J. Landoll is an information security author, consultant, teacher, and business owner. When he is not performing risk assessments or writing policies he is coming up with better approaches and methods and preparing for his next class or book. Follow him on twitter @douglandoll or see what he is up to at www.lantego.com.

Landoll is an information security author, consultant, teacher, and business owner. He is an insightful author who always brings a unique mix of business strategy, technical know-how, and pragmatic approaches to current information security topics. Landoll's first book *The Security Risk Assessment Handbook* (Auerbach, 2006, 2011) is a top seller and now in its second edition due largely to his ability to convey the methods, techniques, and tricks of performing information security consulting.

In his 25+ years in the industry he has coded and evaluated trusted products for the NSA (National Security Agency); assessed vulnerabilities in systems for the CIA (Central Intelligence Agency), FBI (Federal Bureau of Investigation), and NATO (North Atlantic Treaty Organization); built security programs for corporations large and small; guided information security compliance initiatives for regulated industries; instructed over 1500 CISSP (Certified Information Systems Security Professional) and CISA (Certified Information Systems Auditor) candidates; and started and ran four information security companies.

Landoll holds a CISSP, a computer science degree from James Madison University, and an MBA from the University of Texas, Austin. In 2013, Landoll was inducted as a distinguished fellow by the Information Systems Security Association (ISSA).

1

INTRODUCTION

Every organization with information systems or data has a business objective of protecting its critical information systems and sensitive data. In the past, information security protection was viewed as an unknown art practiced by the "techies," but the numerous major breaches and information security events that have taken place have made protection of information systems and data among the top concerns in the C-suite.

In a 2015 survey by PricewaterhouseCoopers, almost 45% of CEOs in the United States rated their level of concern about cyber threats and lack of data security as "extremely concerned." A total of 86% (up from 69% in 2014) of the same executives expressed that they were either "somewhat concerned" or "extremely concerned" about these threats.[*] The appropriate allocation of resources should follow such concerns, yet the security programs of corporations worldwide still lag the concern level and involvement from the top. In another survey by PwC it was observed that involvement from the organization's board was lacking in all activities for the majority of companies surveyed (see Figure 1.1).[†]

Addressing the imbalance between concern and action cannot be handled overnight, so a certain amount of lag is expected. Even among those organizations that do have a reasonable information security program in place, additions and improvements to those programs will be a continuing and evolving program. The basis of any information security program is the involvement of top management and a set of information security policies. Involvement of the top management is required to understand corporate goals and obtain the required

---

[*] 2015 US CEO Survey, Top Findings, PricewaterhouseCoopers LLP, www.pwc.com/us/en/ceo-survey/secure-assets.html.
[†] Managing cyber risks in an interconnected world: key findings from The Global State of Information Security Survey 2015, www.pwc.com/gsiss2015.

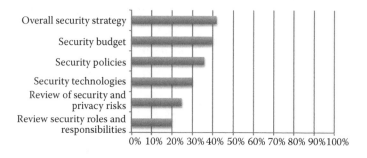

Figure 1.1   Board involvement in key security activities. Board level involvement in key security activities is lacking in most US corporations.

resources and support for the program. Indeed lack of information security policies and security policy awareness have a strong correlation with staff-related breaches. A 2013 survey found that "93% of companies where security policy was poorly understood has staff-related breaches (versus 47% where the policy was well understood)."[*]

The information security policy set is necessary to define the goals and objectives of the information security program. Still many corporations lack a basic and updated set of information security policies. A survey by Protivi found 25% of organizations have no information security policies at all and an even greater percentage have an incomplete information security policy set (see Figure 1.2).[†]

The 2013 PWC Global State of Information Security Survey provides even more details on missing security policy elements of organizations worldwide. The survey found that over half of all organizations missed key security policy elements such as user administration and physical security. In fact, in only one area of security policy, backup and recovery, did over half of the organizations address security policy (and then only 51%) (Figure 1.3).

Even among those organizations with a complete information security policy set, these policies are often ineffective and not consistent

---

[*] 2013 Information Security Breaches Survey: Executive Summary, Department for Business, Innovation and Skills, 2013, www.pwc.co.uk/assets/pdf/cyber-security-2013-exec-summary.pdf.

[†] Knowing How—and Where—Your Confidential Data Is Classified and Managed: A Survey on the Current State of IT Security and Privacy Policies and Practices. Protiviti, 2013, http://www.protiviti.com/en-US/Documents/Surveys/2013-IT-Security-Privacy-Survey-Protiviti.pdf.

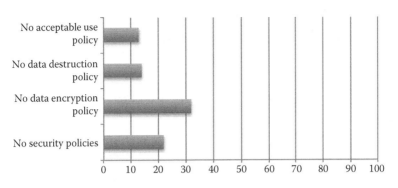

Figure 1.2 Missing information security policies. Many organizations are missing key information security policies; some have none at all.

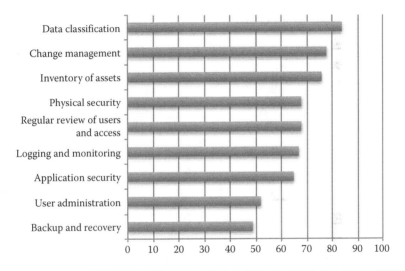

Figure 1.3 Missing security policy elements. Over half of all organizations are missing key security policy elements on all areas reviewed but backup and recovery.

with corporate objectives due to a lack of maintenance and updating of the policy set. A survey conducted by InsightExpress[*] found that information technology (IT) workers indicated that 23% of organizations have no security policies and 76% have ineffective or outdated security policies (Figure 1.4).

Remedying this situation of outdated and incomplete information security policy sets is the focus of this book. Organizations can

---

[*] Data Leakage Worldwide: The Effectiveness of Security Policies, www.cisco.com/c/en/us/solutions/collateral/enterprise-networks/data-loss-prevention/white-paper_c11-503131.pdf.

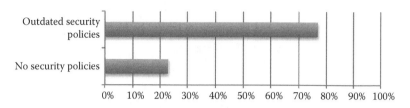

Figure 1.4 State of organizational security policies. Board level involvement in key security activities is lacking in most US corporations.

accomplish vast improvements in their security posture by creating or revising a set of information security policies that identifies and implements the organization's information security objectives.

1.1 No Short Cuts

The creation or revision of an information security policy set is no small task. A complete set of information security policies typically covers a wide array of information security policy subjects and controls (see Table 1.1).

The amount of effort it takes to research, draft, approve, and convey these policies is substantial. There is a temptation to conclude that someone else has done this before and one set of policies is as good as any other. So why not just use templates or buy a set of prewritten policies? While example policies and even prewritten policies offer a good worked example to guide the development of you own information security policies, users should be aware that prewritten policies' claims of "compliance in a box" or "ready-made policies" should be met with a large degree of skepticism and a plan for disappointment. The minimal value and effectiveness of these prewritten 'one-size-fits-all' policies is a generally accepted understanding within the information security community but for clarity, the following reasons are given on why information security policies must be created and tailored for each organization:

- *Business mission.* The first most obvious reason for not succumbing to the temptation of "instant policies" or "policies in a box" is that not all businesses are the same. An information security policy set establishes your organization's security program. To meet business objectives, security must be

Table 1.1 Basic Outline of Information Security Policy Set

POLICY AREA	POLICY SUBJECTS	EXAMPLE ELEMENTS
Rules of behavior	• Security awareness • Acceptable use policy • Sanctions policy • Hiring and termination policy	• Training, topics • Expected and prohibited behavior • Discipline process • Employee screening, account termination
Roles and responsibilities	• Information security officer • Information security manager • System owner • Data owner • System custodian	• Overall responsibility for security • Functional responsibility for security in department • Defines system security • Defines data security • Implements security
Minimum security controls	Administrative	• Account management • Business continuity planning • Disaster recovery • Incident response
	Physical	• Workplace security • Workstation, laptop, and removable media security • Sensitive area security
	Technical	• Network controls • Server controls • Application controls • Device controls • Transmission controls
Oversight	• Monitoring • Assessment • Audit • Testing	• Sensors, metrics • Risk assessment • Account right review • Vulnerability scanning, penetration testing

Note: Information security policy sets cover a wide array of information security controls.

consistent with business objectives, be cost effective, and provide a business advantage to the organization.

- *Organization structure.* Information security policies must establish and convey explicit information security responsibilities, accountability, and oversight for your organization's structure.
- *Organizational controls.* An effective information security program is well integrated into the rest of the organization's processes and controls. For example, an incident response policy and procedure must be integrated into security awareness, acceptable use policies, sanctions, help desk and ticketing

information systems, disaster recovery plans, and breach notification procedures.

- *Industry, threats, and culture.* All information security policy
sets address (or at least should) many of the same issues, but
the strength of the control, the strictness of the sanction, and
the degree of oversight in these controls must fit the organization's threat environment, industry, and company culture.

This book contains numerous examples of policy statements and
even a complete information security policy set. These examples and
example set are for illustrative purposes to show depth-of-control
description, example formats, and an example policy set framework.
They are not intended as a replacement for solid information security
engineering and policy writing.

1.2 Top-Down Security

When embarking on the creation or revision of an information security policy set, it is important to remember that top management
involvement in the security program and the creation of information
security policies go hand in hand.

> Information security policies are the statement of top management
> intent on how to protect information systems and ensure the security
> and privacy of sensitive data.

The approach of defining and implementing security controls based
on the directions of top management (reflecting business objectives) is
called "top-down security."

Organizations implementing their information security programs in a top-down manner benefit from a security program that is
designed to meet the business (or mission) objectives through a clear
understanding of the sensitive data and critical information systems
(i.e., assets) that support their mission, the threats to these assets, the
potential vulnerabilities in the information systems and controls, and
a well-designed information security program that effectively uses
corporate resources to protect these assets appropriately.

Unfortunately, not all information security programs are developed using the top-down security approach. Without this strategic

direction, security programs tend to develop from the bottom-up. Rather than an intentional security program created from mission objectives, the management intent on those responsible for the operational protection must make daily decisions based on their own understanding of potential threats and the need to protect corporate assets. Bottom-up security programs evolve in the vacuum of strategy based on perceived technology needs or a daily reaction to issues as they are discovered rather than to review the system of controls that may have led to this vulnerability (e.g., patch management, system configuration standards, configuration management, account provisioning, account monitoring, and account rights reviews. When confronted with a serious vulnerability such as nonapplication of a critical patch in an existing system or a dormant administrative account, the immediate reaction is to patch the vulnerability and move on to the next task. Information security programs that lack strategic direction or documentation tend to mirror this "penetrate-patch-and-proceed" approach. The result is a technology-heavy program that is limited in that it addresses security symptoms discovered at the staff level.

While the discovery of security issues at the staff level is an important part of any security monitoring and incident response capability, an information security program operating without high-level direction and decisions is misaligned with the organizational business objectives. The "bottom-up approach" to security may seem to be a more direct approach to the known organizational information systems and control issues, but this misalignment with the organizational mission degrades the program and leads to many inefficient uses of organizational resources such as staff-level risk decisions, symptom-based remediation, a noncompliant security program, lack of adoption of a security program, and lack of awareness of security controls and procedures.

Staff-level risk decisions are security-risk decisions made at the information system administrator level and not by corporate officers. Information system administrators are closer to many of the security-risk issues and often have a better technical understanding of the control, vulnerability, or countermeasure, but the security risk is to the organization and the decisions on how to deal with it are organizational and not operational decisions. Many components go into an understanding of discovered risks and determining the appropriate organizational response, including impact to other organizational departments, the reporting structures, regulation and contract compliance, customer requirements, potential legal and reporting requirements, and the organization's risk aversion. Staff-level risk decisions may seem a more direct response but ultimately put the organization at a greater security risk.

Symptom-based remediation happens when technology and countermeasures deployed to address the symptoms of discovered vulnerabilities fail to address the underlying issues. Consider an organization that has a penetration test performed and discovers that one of its web servers has not been patched in 6 months and is vulnerable to a well-known attack. The recommendation from the penetration test typically states that the information system should be updated to include the vendor patch that addresses the issue. The staff-level response typically follows this recommendation and moves on. This approach is sometimes referred to as the "penetrate-patch-and-proceed" process and can lead to a steady state of a consistently vulnerable information system because the solution focused only on the symptom. The likelihood of a similar vulnerability existing in another server 6 months from now has not been addressed or reduced. Consider instead the top-down approach that includes other organizational elements, the analysis of nontechnical potential controls, and the search for a root cause. Recommendations coming from an organizational approach to security risks (instead of limiting them to technical solutions) could reveal the root cause to be a lack of training, the need for configuration standards, oversight and governance controls, or improved accountability measures.

Another major issue with the bottom-up approach is a noncompliant security program. This results when the corporate security program is not demonstrably compliant with regulations or customer requirements, which happens more often in the bottom-up approach because regulations and customer requirements are by their very nature a top-down approach. Information security regulations (e.g., Health Insurance Portability and Accountability Act Security and Privacy Rules) are a set of required controls for your organization to follow based on the sensitivity of data entrusted to the organization or the criticality of the organization's information systems. The regulation requirements become codified in your organization through your own set of security policies and procedures that ensure appropriate protection of sensitive data and critical information systems. These controls are rarely limited to technical controls. Relegation of regulation compliance to the staff level results in an incomplete approach to addressing the required controls and a noncompliant security program.

Any heroic or individual efforts to lock down critical information systems and safeguard sensitive data are likely to remain individual efforts. Without a general knowledge and adoption of a set of policies and standards, the organization's information security program cannot be a concerted effort.

Ask any security administrator or staff member how certain security controls are implemented or what activities are prohibited on the system. If they are unaware of the control implementation or expected behavior, then it is clear that information security policy and procedure awareness is lacking. When those expected to implement controls or behave appropriately on the organization's system are unaware of the rules, these information systems are vulnerable.

Given the weaknesses of the bottom-up approach to building and maintaining information security programs, organizations should adopt the top-down approach. This approach is based on clear articulation of the information security strategy based on organizational objectives, the effective communication of the security program goals, and allocation of responsibilities in carrying out those goals; in short, information security policies, procedures, and standards—the establishment and management of an information security program utilizing a well-structured set of information security policies, procedures, and standards. These policies, procedures, and standards are to be developed as a direct extension of the organizational mission. An organizationally aligned information security program is the effective use of organizational resources and has several benefits including relevance to organizational mission, program completeness, process maturity, governance and oversight, planning and budget support, and audit and compliance support.

To be aligned with the organizational mission, an information security program must be defined and managed through a set of information security policies, procedures, and standards derived from an understanding of the organizational mission. Specific mission elements that affect the information security policies, procedures, and standards include the corporate structure, competitive positioning, customer commitment, and industry vertical.

Information security programs built from the top-down should be based on a security framework (e.g., NIST 800-53, ISO 27001/2, or COBIT). These frameworks provide a structured method to organize and reason the security objectives and controls needed to implement appropriate protection.

As an organization's information security program matures, it is important to understand that well-understood and implemented administrative processes provide a far more consistent and effective protection of organizational assets than the standard "hero" approach. This approach is the belief that smart people will do smart things. The problem with this approach is that it lacks discipline and repeatability. Smart people are capable of smart actions but seldom are those actions consistent, always performed, or repeatable. When defending your assets and information systems repeatability trumps occasionally clever.

Assigning a responsibility to someone is one thing, but ensuring that the responsibility is met is governance and oversight. Immature and hero-based information security programs can have many information security controls in place but their implementation can be spotty and ineffective when governance and oversight controls are lacking. A top-down flow of responsibilities and oversight is an important element of designing the information security program, and this is implemented through the development of an information security policy, procedures, and standards set.

Information security programs are not static. They need to continually evolve and react to changing environments and threats. Changing the program requires planning and the procurement of organizational funds for additional controls. The information security policy, procedures, and standards set can be used as a planning and budget tool. Gaining senior management support for information security spending is far more effective when addressing a policy gap because the policy was developed to be consistent with organizational needs.

Finally, an information security program based on a solid information security policy set is a required element of any information security audit or compliance program. If your organization is required to undergo information security audits, information security regulations audits, or information security compliance reviews, it is the information security policy set that forms the definition of your security program. An auditor's mantra is "if its not documented—it's not done"

Table 1.2   Benefits of Top-Down Security

BENEFITS OF TOP-DOWN SECURITY	PROBLEMS WITH BOTTOM-UP SECURITY
• Mission relevance	• Symptom-based risk management
• Program completeness	• Staff-level risk decisions
• Process maturity	• Noncompliant security program
• Governance and oversight	• Lack of adoption
• Planning and budget support	• Lack of awareness
• Audit and compliance support	

Note: Information security programs are best implemented in a top-down design. Top-down security means that information security controls are derived from organizational mission objectives.

may be a bit of an exaggeration. Closer to the truth would be "if its not documented—its done not consistently" (Table 1.2).

Organizations seeking a strong information security program, improvements in their existing program, or an effective approach to compliance, governance, and oversight should first look into their information security policy set. Information security policies, procedures, and standards play a key role in defining and maintaining the corporate information security program. In order to align the implementation of the security program to the business objectives, the information security program must be planned, documented, implemented, monitored, and maintained. Information security policies, procedures, and standards are the definition of the corporate information security program and the documentation of such an alignment.

1.3 Current State of Information Security Policy Sets

The value of this text would be suspected if most organizations had a strong information security policy set. The fact is that among all of the elements of an effective information security program, the information security policy set is the one control with the most room for improvement for most organizations. The good news is that you are reading this text, and improvements in this area are likely to result in major improvements to your security program.

The information security policies set for many organizations remain ineffective because they are nonexistent, inaccurate, ignored, or unclear. In several recent surveys [Cisco_1], [Protivit_1], it has been determined that around 23% of corporations do not have any information security policies—not an outdated or incomplete policy set, but a complete lack of any information security policies. Clearly those organizations are exhibiting bottom-up security. Creation of an information security policy set would provide vast improvements in the effectiveness and manageability of their information security program.

For those organizations that do have a written information security policy, many of these policies are not well integrated into the information security practices and are largely ignored (i.e., shelfware). An information security policy set that does not govern and provide guidance over the implementation of security controls has likely been created in support of an audit, regulation compliance, or customer request but was never truly adopted by the organization. These policies typically have derived from "standard industry templates" and have little to no effect on the implementation and governance of security controls. The organization envisioned a documented security program to inform users of acceptable behaviors and documented the workflow of critical processes; however, the implementation of a complete but nonintegrated information security policy has little effect on the security program.

Information security policy templates and examples are great ways to demonstrate how these documents may be formatted, the depth of the control descriptions, and key document sections. A security policy author working for an organization may use templates as a way to research or as worked examples, but these documents should be used with caution. Never substitute a worked example for an analysis of the organization's mission, requirements, environment, and capabilities. For information security policies, procedures, and standards to be effectively integrated and used within an organization, these documents must match the business processes and needs of the organization. Any security policy author who simply modifies a security policy template by inserting his/her name in the "[Organization]" field is creating a nonintegrated policy set. Templates may provide a useful document structure but when the contents are not analyzed and tailored for the organization, the result is a policy that does not affect the security program and does not meet the intent of the regulations, requirements, or the business mission.

Other organizations have at one time initiated and completed an information security policy program in which they created an information security policy set that meets their needs. As part of this effort, the policies reflected their current organization, technology, regulations, and the threat environment. However, aside from minor edits, these policies have gone unchanged for 3–5 years (or more). There are some telltale signs of outdated and out-of-touch policies such as the document date, and those documents that still reference PDAs and do not reference smart phones or social media are out of date. Other policy sets are outdated in less obvious ways such as referencing and implementing older versions of regulations or assigning responsibilities to departments that have been renamed or consolidated. Such policies are not only outdated but inconsistent with organizational goals.

It should be rather obvious that outdated policies have now fallen into the category of "largely ignored." By referencing old technology, not providing relevant technology guidance, not addressing current threats, and being inconsistent with the organizational structure, these policies cease to provide direction and are not used to implement or monitor the organization's information security program.

Finally, many information security policy sets can be difficult to understand. Even well-meaning users seeking to understand the rules governing the use of corporate resources cannot figure out what actions are allowed or restricted. These information security policies typically suffer from a lack of organization, consistency, and clarity of language.

Common problems in these types of information security policy sets include the following issues:

- *Prose instead of policy.* Users can gain information about specific technologies, regulations, and threats in the security awareness training or from company bulletins. When users consult a policy to see whether they need to encrypt a flash drive and with what algorithm and key strength, it should be a simple process. Instead users are many times treated to a two to three paragraph discussion of the threats. A policy statement is typically buried within those paragraphs for the user to find and abide by, but many times it is lost in a sea of prose. The result is an unclear policy and one that no longer serves the purpose of providing the rules in a clear and concise manner, and therefore, no longer consulted for direction and requirements.

- *Mixed policy and procedures.* An information security policy is a statement of management intent with respect to the protection and treatment of information assets. This is the "what" of the information security program. An example information security policy statement is "all information systems shall be hardened prior to being released into production." A procedure is step-by-step instruction on the implementation of one or more policy statements. This is the "how" of the information security program. An example of an information security procedure would detail the approach taken to harden a specific technology such as "the following steps are implemented to harden a web server." When policy statements and procedure statements are mixed in a single document, the message becomes cumbersome and confused.
- *Mixed audience.* In addition to the mixed message example above, the audience for the single document is inappropriate. Informing users or customers that information systems are hardened is appropriate but the method in which the hardening is implemented may be sensitive and not releasable to all users or customers.

1.4 Effectiveness of Information Security Policy Sets

Many in the information security industry have long viewed information security policies as less than effective. It is not unusual to hear those in IT state, "policies do not enforce anything; it takes technology to really implement security." The thought here is that policies are not active or effective security controls. Whereas, a firewall can actively block a packet sent to the network that does not meet certain requirements, policy statements such as "do not take pictures in the data center" can simply be ignored.

There is no denying that policies are passive but there are several key fallacies in the "policies do not enforce anything" argument. First, the information security policies themselves are passive but the activities they define to be performed are active. Information security policies typically require activities such as visitor escorts, code reviews, account rights reviews, and other information security activities that do actively enforce a security control. In fact, without policies and procedures these controls are rarely performed or done in a consistent manner.

Second, the overwhelming majority of employees and contractors will obey security policies and procedures if they are made aware of them. Security policies are the statement of the management goals and objectives for the security program, information system security, and user behavior. Most employees and contractors will operate within the rules of the organization and the information system but those rules must first be clear. For example, when I visit a new client and I arrive onsite, I respect the organization's wishes on how I am to behave. If I am presented with an acceptable use policy or a visitor code of conduct, then I am aware of the rules that govern my behavior. Many times I am offered no such policies leaving me unaware of any unexpected rules that may govern how I am to behave (i.e., no camera phones on the premises, or visitors must be escorted). Without providing these policies to visitors, contractors, and staff, the policies are very likely to not have much effect on the behavior of individuals. However, if these policies are provided and incorporated into contracting and security awareness training, they are very effective at informing these people and influencing behavior. In a recent study comparing organizations with various levels of security policy awareness, it was found that "93% of companies where security policy was poorly understood had staff-related breaches (vs. 47% where the policy was well understood)" [PWC_1].

Finally, information security policies are the definition of an organization's information security program. Without information security policies and procedures, there is no planned, documented, and managed set of information security controls. The 2013 ISC2 Global Workforce study found that three of the top four categories for securing infrastructure are security policy related. Topping the list of important components of a security program was management support of security policies (with 89% ranked as important or very important), third on the list was "adherence to security policy" (86%), and fourth on the list was training of staff on security policy (83%).*

* The 2013 ISC2 Global Information Security Workforce Study, Frost & Sullivan, https://www.isc2cares.org/uploadedFiles/wwwisc2caresorg/Content/2013-ISC2-Global-Information-Security-Workforce-Study.pdf.

EXERCISES

1. Information security controls can be planned and implemented from a top-down or bottom-up perspective.
   a. Compare and contrast top-down security and bottom-up security.
   b. Describe a situation where bottom-up security is more advantageous.
   c. Why is top-down security generally more appropriate for the creation of information security policies?
2. How does an information security policy framework assist in the top-down implementation of information security policy frameworks?
3. Review your own organization's information security policies for currency and applicability.
   a. Can you identify when they were last updated? Is this a reasonable time?
   b. Can you identify upon which information security regulations, laws, and standards the current set of policies are based? Is this inclusive of the required regulations for your industry and sensitive data within your information systems?
   c. Be prepared to discuss how information security policies dictate user behavior in your organization and why.
   d. Be prepared to discuss how information security policies dictate information system security controls in your organization and why.

2

INFORMATION SECURITY POLICY BASICS

Information security policy is the general term referring to any document that conveys an element of the security program in order to enforce organizational security goals and objectives. Since this definition covers such a wide array of security policy documents, it is useful to describe the various types of information security policies that an organization may employ.

The terms used below to describe these information security policy types are in general use within the information security industry and will be used consistently throughout this chapter. However, it is not unusual for a specific organization or government agency to have alternative names for the same information security policy types. For example, in many organizations and certainly in government departments, the word "policy" is closely associated with laws and regulations. In these cases, a limited number of people (e.g., legislature) have the authority to create policy, so an information security policy is typically referred to by other names such as "information security statement," or "information security document" or other terms avoiding the use of the word "policy." The term an organization uses to describe these documents does not matter. The general organization and completeness of these documents does matter.

2.1 Information Security Policy Types

In this chapter, we use the terms policy, standard, procedure, baseline, and guidelines to describe the various information security policy document types. The structure and organization of these information security policy types are illustrated in Figure 2.1.

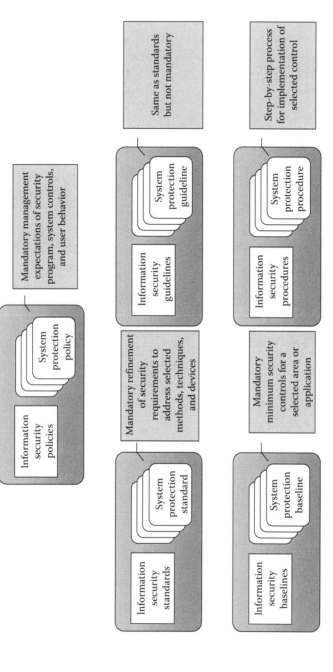

Figure 2.1 Information security policy types. Information security policy documents are implemented at various levels of detail and typically referred to as policies, standards, procedures, baselines, and guidelines.

2.1.1 Information Security Policies

Information security policies are the highest level of information security policy sets. These policies are approved and issued by the senior management of the organization as their expectations for the overall security program, system controls, and user behavior. Information security policies are mandatory in that all information systems and users are expected to conform to the policy statements. An example policy statement may read: "The organization shall ensure that all information systems implement authentication with sufficient strength of mechanism for their intended use."

Within this top level of the information security policy, documents are various policies directed at the organizational level, the security program level, the user level, and the system level. Figure 2.2 illustrates the four levels of information security policies, namely, organizational, security program, user, and system levels.

Organizational level information security policies address the overall information security program and the sensitivity of data. In Information Security Program policy, senior management dictates the required elements of the information security program, assigns responsibilities, and establishes oversight controls. In the Data and System Classification Policy, senior management defines levels of

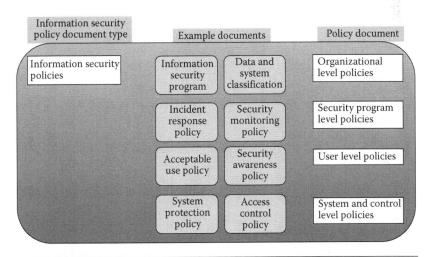

Figure 2.2 Information security policy levels—example. Within the top level of information security policy types are various types of policies addressing an associated group of controls such as organizational, security program, users, and system controls.

classification for both data and information systems based on the sensitivity of the data and the criticality of the system. Along with the classification definitions, senior management establishes minimum controls for the sensitive data (e.g., handlings, labeling, transportation, and destruction) and the process by which information systems will be secured and managed based on the system classification level.

Each of these individual policy types is listed and briefly described here as an example of the four levels of the information security policies.

2.1.2 Information Security Standards

Information security standards are a refinement of security requirements in the information security policies that address selected methods, techniques, and devices. These standards are mandatory as they specify required refinements of the information security policies. Standards are typically issued and approved by either senior management or their delegates such as an information security officer or information security manager.

An example standard statement may read: "The organization shall ensure that for password-based authentication, all information systems enforce the following minimum parameter settings: (a) password complexity—8 characters with both numeric and alphabetic characters, (b) password lifetime—60 days maximum, 1 day minimum, (c) password reuse—6 generations."

Information security standards are developed to provide greater explanation or specificity for information security policy level statements. For this reason, information security standards should have a direct and clear correlation to the information security policy statement they are refining. One approach in ensuring this correlation is to create an information security standard with the same root name as the information security policy. For example, the information security policy document "System Protection Policy" would have a corresponding information security standard document "System Protection Standard." Within the standard, each standard requirement would be clearly linked (e.g., same numbering scheme and requirement titles) to the corresponding information security policy statement it is refining.

2.1.3 Information Security Guidelines

Information security guidelines are also a refinement of security requirements in the information security policies that address selected methods, techniques, and devices. These guidelines are written just like standards but they are not mandatory as they specify suggested refinements of the information security policies. Guidelines are typically issued and approved by either senior management or their delegates such as an information security officer or information security manager. As these are not mandatory, it is not unusual to have the guidelines authored and shared without a formal approval process. In these cases, subject matter experts may create, publish, and share guidelines.

An example guideline statement may read: "The organization *should* ensure that for password-based authentication, all information systems enforce the following minimum parameter settings: (a) password complexity—8 characters with both numeric and alphabetic characters, (b) password lifetime—60 days maximum, 1 day minimum, (c) password reuse—6 generations."

Information security guidelines should be created to show the same direct correlation to information security policies as the standards. The same naming convention and document structure approach is recommended. For example, the information security policy document "System Protection Policy" would have a corresponding information security guideline document "System Protection Guideline." Within the guideline document, each guideline statement would be clearly linked (e.g., same numbering scheme and requirement titles) to the corresponding information security policy statement it is refining.

2.1.4 Information Security Baselines

Information security baselines (also called benchmarks) are mandatory minimum-security controls for a selected area or application. They are also a refinement of security requirements in the information security policies but they are used for devices, applications, or other areas where a number of settings, parameters, and activities are related to the effectiveness of a security control. An example guideline statement may read, when deploying a browser within the production environment organizations shall implement the associated United States Government Configuration Baseline (USGCB) for the browser. The USGCB is a configuration baseline for various operating information systems and applications and covers security settings and parameters for the specific application.*

Baselines typically involve a large number of settings and parameters based on known vulnerabilities within the application. As new vulnerabilities are discovered, the baseline is updated to reflect the best approach for reducing the security risk within the application. Many organizations lack the resources necessary to perform the research necessary to keep baselines up to date and will instead rely on external organizations to create and maintain baselines. Several organizations that produce and maintain baselines include the National Institute of Standards and Technology, the Center for Internet Security, and information security product vendors.

Information security baselines should be created for each device, application, or other area in which a set of minimum-security controls and settings would be useful to the organization.

2.1.5 Information Security Procedures

Information security procedures are step-by-step instructions for the implementation of security controls or processes dictated in the information security policies, standards, guidelines, or baselines. They are also a refinement of security requirements in the information security policies but they provide the "how" and the "who." For example, an information security procedure in support of an account management/account initialization policy or standard would provide detailed instructions and screenshots for how an account would be created, assigned rights, and communicated to the user.

The act of documenting procedures creates a common approach and understanding among the various roles and individuals implementing and interfacing with the process. For many procedures, multiple roles are involved in various aspects of the tasks. For example, a termination procedure involves the employee, his or her supervisor, human resources, information technology, finance, and, potentially, legal. Documenting the tasks involved with this process, their order, and the roles and responsibilities of the parties involved assures understanding not only individual roles but also how others contribute to the process.

---

* http://usgcb.nist.gov/.

EXERCISES

1. Briefly explain the difference between a policy, standard, guideline, procedure, and baseline.
2. What are the benefits of documenting security procedures (e.g., account provisioning)?
3. Consider an organization that has outsourced system configuration to a cloud services provider for those servers in the cloud.
    a. How would you go about documenting your organization's policy for system configuration in a cloud environment if a third party managed the configuration?
    b. How would you go about documenting your organization's procedures for system configuration in a cloud environment if a third party managed the configuration?

3

INFORMATION SECURITY POLICY FRAMEWORK

Developing and maintaining a set of documents that make up the information security policy set (e.g., policy, standards, guidelines, and procedures) for an organization can be a significant undertaking. These documents cover the goals, objectives, and requirements for the organization's security program, user behavior, and minimum controls for information systems and applications. To say such a document set results in a large set of policy statements is an understatement.

To provide some structure to this process, it is imperative that the author or project leader of the information security policy set adopts a framework to guide the development and ensure proper coverage. A framework is simply the basic structure of a system. The careful and solid creation of any complex system without an underlying framework or structure is difficult if not impossible. In the context of information security policies, a framework is the basic structure of the various policies, procedures, and standards. The importance of a system structure (e.g., information security policy framework [ISPF]) is to ensure that the system created is sound by providing an approach for consideration of all essential elements and a way to reason about how those elements relate and support each other.

3.1 Information Security Policy Sets without Frameworks

Before discussing various information SPFs available to pattern the development of your own information security policy set, it may be useful to discuss the importance of adopting a framework at all. Indeed many information security policy sets in effect at organizations today lack the structure of a framework. Such policy sets suffer organization, clarity, and are a nightmare to maintain. The following two examples illustrate some difficulties that are sometimes experienced with information security policy sets derived without the structure of a framework:

- *Referencing the information security policy set.* When asked whether an organization has a stance on a specific behavior or control, many people within the organization are quick to conclude that there is a policy on that topic, but when pressed to find the policy statement, they many times are unable to find a reference in their policy set. For example, ask yourself or your customer whether they have a policy against cell phones with video recording capabilities in a data center or whether they have a data classification policy. If they believe that such a policy exists ask them to bring up the reference. Many times they will find that it is difficult to find where in the policies such a control would be discussed. Furthermore, many times these controls will simply be missing or simply discussed at a high level with no specific controls (e.g., data classification without handling restrictions associated to various levels).

- *Updating the information security policy set.* Given an organization's existing information security policy set consider the addition of recent changes to an information security regulation that applied to the organization (e.g., Health Insurance Portability and Accountability Act [HIPAA] and Payment Card Industry Data Security Standard [PCI DSS]). How difficult would it be to first identify the policy statements that implemented the previous version of the information security regulation? Now how difficult would it be to implement the changes to the information security regulation throughout the information security policy set? These information security policy sets are typically updated by adding yet another policy for every new topic.

An information security policy set that is difficult to reference, or even find the relevant policy statements regarding a security topic or concern, is not serving the objective of guiding behavior and establishing minimum controls. An information security policy set that is difficult to update or support an audit against a specific regulation is equally ineffective. By continually adding to the information security policy set simply because it is too difficult to find the previous policy statements regarding similar and related controls, the information security policy set becomes more confused, conflicting, and unrelated to the real information security strategy of the organization. The adoption of an ISPF addresses these concerns and provides other benefits as well.

3.2 Information Security Policy Sets with Frameworks

The benefits of a structured information security policy set based on a framework include usefulness, audit support, and maintainability. The structure of an information security policy has many advantages:

- *Completeness.* An ISPF is organized to demonstrate complete coverage of the relevant areas affected by information security policies (e.g., people, process, and technology). By adopting an ISPF, the organization is assured that the policy set provides coverage for the relevant areas that require guidance for information security controls. Adoption of an ISPF provides a more complete information security policy set.
- *Consistency.* An information security policy set organized according to a framework requires grouping of associated controls (e.g., passwords, patch management, or audit review). By grouping related controls (e.g., password strength and password expiration) and all references to these controls in a single portion of the policy set, it is easier to ensure consistency throughout the information security policy set for a specific control. In other words, it is less likely that one policy will require six character passwords, whereas another policy requires eight characters.
- *Compliance.* The structure of the information security policy set, when structured based on a framework, can assist in information security compliance efforts. Most information security frameworks have mappings (or "crosswalks") to relevant information security regulations. Demonstrating compliance with the documentation (policies and procedures) elements of information security regulations is aided greatly by these mappings.
- *Common mapping.* Information security policy sets based on common frameworks are also based on common or industry accepted mappings to other frameworks, regulations, and

technologies. The mapping of information security program requirements to information security projects and technology procurement becomes an essential element of maturing the information security program.

- *Improved use and understanding.* Information security policy sets organized and based on frameworks improve the integration of the various policies by providing an understanding of basic elements and their interaction. First, policy statements are grouped according to their topic areas and audiences. For example, a user seeking to understand his or her expected behavior on the corporate network does not need to consult the software usage policy, the security awareness training, the network usage policy, and the Bring Your Own Device policy. Instead all users' expected behavior can be a single section in the Acceptable Use Policy. Second, references to other policy statements such as the encryption policy statements are easy and succinct because all encryption policy statements can be referenced in a single reference to the encryption policy.

3.3 Common Information SPFs

Given the benefits of using an ISPF on which to base an organization's information security policy set, organizations should strive to adopt a framework for their information security policy project. There are many available frameworks upon which to build and maintain an information security policy set.

The more useful frameworks are generally well accepted within the industry, up to date with advances (e.g., threats and controls) in the industry, and well structured to support their use. There are several information security (or even information technology [IT]) frameworks that meet these framework requirements and should be considered when adopting a framework for the development and maintenance of an information security policy set. These frameworks include the Federal Information Security Management Act (FISMA), the International Standards Organization (ISO) 27001/2:2013, Control Objectives for Information and Related Technology (COBIT), and the Her Majesty's Government (HMG) ISPF. There are certainly plenty of other SPFs that have been adopted and may work well for your organization but a description of these SPFs is adequate to illustrate the usefulness and importance of adopting a framework.

3.3.1 FISMA Framework

The FISMA, enacted in 2002, requires federal departments, government contractors, and government service providers to implement and manage an information security program. The federal information security program requirements are defined in the FISMA Implementation Project by the publications authored by the National Institute of Standards and Technology (NIST). Table 3.1 provides a summary of the major documents of the FISMA Implementation Project.

The core document of the FISMA project is Special Publication (SP) 800-53: Security and Privacy Controls for Information Systems and Organizations. Although this document is intended as a catalog of security and privacy controls, the basic structure and organization of these requirements provides a useful framework for the organization and construction of information security policies.

Table 3.1 FISMA Implementation Project Documents

NIST SPECIAL PUBLICATION	TITLE	DESCRIPTION
FIPS 199	Standards for security categorization of federal information and information systems	Mandatory federal standard for determining the security category of information systems
FIPS 200	Minimum security requirements for federal information and information systems	Mandatory federal standard for deriving the impact level from the security category for information systems
SP 800-53	Security and privacy controls for federal information systems and organizations	Federal guideline for selecting the minimum-security controls for information systems and the organization
FIPS 140-2	Security requirements for cryptographic modules	Federal standard for the specification of cryptographic-based security information systems used to protect sensitive data Also established the cryptographic module validation program for the validation of cryptographic modules by cryptographic and security testing laboratories
FIPS 140-3 DRAFT	Security requirements for cryptographic modules	Proposed revision for FIPS 140-2

Note: The FISMA Implementation Project was established in 2003 as a result of the Federal Information Security Management Act (FISMA). The NIST defined the minimum-security requirements for federal information systems processing sensitive data through this program.

Table 3.2   FISMA Control Families

ID	CONTROL FAMILY	ID	CONTROL FAMILY
AC	Access control	MP	Media protection
AT	Awareness and training	PE	Physical and environmental protection
AU	Audit and accountability	PL	Planning
CA	Security assessment and authorization	PS	Personnel security
CM	Configuration management	RA	Risk assessment
CP	Contingency planning	SA	System and services acquisition
IA	Identification and authentication	SC	System and communication protection
IR	Incident response	SI	System and information integrity
MA	Maintenance	PM	Program management

Note: The information security and privacy controls listed in NIST SP 800-53 are organized into families and identified with a digraph.

The information security and privacy controls described in the NIST SP 800-53 document are well defined and organized. Each of the controls belongs to one of 18 control families. The security control families are listed in Table 3.2, along with their digraph identifier.

Within each control family is a hierarchical set of control requirements intended for low-, moderate-, and high-impact information systems. Briefly, a system is determined to be high, moderate, or low impact based on the confidentiality, integrity, and availability requirements of the system and the sensitivity of the data (see Federal Information Processing Standard [FIPS] 199 for more detail). These impact ratings are used as the basis for the selection of minimum controls for an organization's system. Depending on the impact rating of the system the controls subset is selected (e.g., all low-impact controls for low-impact information systems; all low- and moderate-impact controls for moderate information systems; and high, moderate, and low controls for high-impact information systems).

Each control requirement is sequentially numbered within the control family (e.g., AC-1, AC-2). Each of these requirements can have additional protection measures called enhancements (e.g., AC-2 (1), AC-2 (2)). These enhancements cover subtopics of the controls requirement such as AC-2 is the control family identification and sequential number identifier for the account management requirement; AC-2 (1) is the identifier for the automated system account management enhancement and AC-2 (2) is the identifier for the removal of temporary accounts enhancement.

3.3.1.1 Using the FISMA Framework as a Policy Framework   Some of the FISMA requirements are high-level requirements that describe security program requirements whereas others are lower-level requirements more suited for system control requirements or even standards. There are two basic approaches to creating an information security policy set based on an existing framework.

- *Framework-Matched Policy Set*: Some frameworks are organized to support a matching policy set. Information security policy sets based on these frameworks are called framework-matched policy sets. Frameworks that support these policy sets are based on either high level or low level requirements.

  A good example of a high-level framework is the HMG Security Policy Framework (SPF). The HMG SPF is not populated with detailed information security controls such as password requirements and account management process elements. Since detailed security requirements are not already allocated to the framework elements there is usually not much to go on and the policy writer will be required to determine the controls, processes, technology, and techniques that must be in place to meet the policy objectives.

  A good example of a low-level framework is the ISO 27001/2 Framework. The ISO 27001//2 framework not only has a high-level set of information security control groups but also a set of allocated information security requirements that do lend themselves to an organization that makes sense within an information security policy set. Many of the embedded controls within each area offer the policy writer a low-level structure in which to create policy content.

  The organization of a framework-matched policy set will be completely dictated by the framework and have the same number of policies as the framework has high-level divisions (see Section 3.3.4 HMG Framework Security Policy Framework, and section 3.3.2 ISO 27001/2 Policy Framework).

  The creation of a framework-matched policy set begins with the creation of a policy matched to each of the framework areas such as "Technology and Services." For each of these areas, the policy writer may utilize the available information from the framework to create policy statements that meet the objectives of each area.

Framework-matched policy sets offer an easy and straight-forward framework of policies (e.g., policy titles). Depending on the depth of the framework, the policy writer may have to take a do-it-yourself style of policy element creation or may be able to rely on the framework to provide a lower-level organization and structure.

SIDEBAR: KEY WORD ANALYSIS

A method used to identify the lower-level structure is to review the framework documents for key words that identify the need for documentation. These key words may vary from framework to framework but should be readily identifiable. An example of a key word analysis is provided in Tables 3.4 and 3.5. Within ISO 27001/2, the following key words were identified as a signal that the control required written policy, procedure, or standard (see Tables 3.4 and 3.5):

- Defined (diagrams)
- Defined (agreement)
- Documented, developed, designed, or formal (procedures)
- Documented (requirements)
- Established (responsibility)
- Established (rules)
- Formal process

- *Framework-Inspired Policy Set*: Some frameworks not only provide a high-level organization of information security controls but also detailed requirements on controls, processes, technology, and techniques. These individual requirements provide the information security policy writer with specific requirements to populate each of the information security policies. However, the organization of these detailed requirements are not completely aligned with the objectives of creating an organized and clear information security policy set. For example, within the FISMA framework the first control for each control family (e.g., AC-1) requires that the organization develop, document, and disseminate policies and procedures (for that specific control family objective). An information security policy set is better organized and more clear when the requirement for the development, documentation, and dissemination for an information security policy set is discussed in a single policy requirement and typically would be part of an information security program policy.

Not all of the specific requirements are organized to accommodate the creation of a well-organized policy. The organization of a framework-inspired policy set will be based on the framework but modified where appropriate. Reorganization of some of the policy elements may be necessary to group like policy elements and create clarity and consistency within the policies and policy set. Examples of modifications to the security framework organization to accommodate a well-organized policy can be seen in Figures 3.1 and 3.2 (FISMA-Based ISPF and ISO 27001/2-based ISPF).

A simple approach to creating an information security policy set based on the FISMA controls would be to create an information security

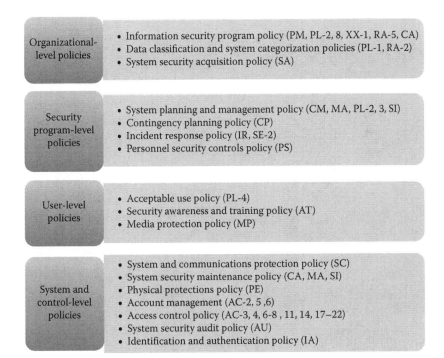

Figure 3.1 FISMA-based ISPF—example. FISMA security controls, as documented in NIST SP 800-53, can be allocated to the four information security policy levels into 17 policies. The policy titles and associated control families, or controls, are listed to the right.

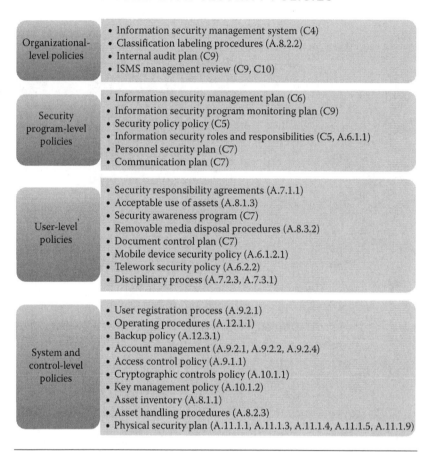

Organizational-level policies	• Information security management system (C4) • Classification labeling procedures (A.8.2.2) • Internal audit plan (C9) • ISMS management review (C9, C10)
Security program-level policies	• Information security management plan (C6) • Information security program monitoring plan (C9) • Security policy policy (C5) • Information security roles and responsibilities (C5, A.6.1.1) • Personnel security plan (C7) • Communication plan (C7)
User-level policies	• Security responsibility agreements (A.7.1.1) • Acceptable use of assets (A.8.1.3) • Security awareness program (C7) • Removable media disposal procedures (A.8.3.2) • Document control plan (C7) • Mobile device security policy (A.6.1.2.1) • Telework security policy (A.6.2.2) • Disciplinary process (A.7.2.3, A.7.3.1)
System and control-level policies	• User registration process (A.9.2.1) • Operating procedures (A.12.1.1) • Backup policy (A.12.3.1) • Account management (A.9.2.1, A.9.2.2, A.9.2.4) • Access control policy (A.9.1.1) • Cryptographic controls policy (A.10.1.1) • Key management policy (A.10.1.2) • Asset inventory (A.8.1.1) • Asset handling procedures (A.8.2.3) • Physical security plan (A.11.1.1, A.11.1.3, A.11.1.4, A.11.1.5, A.11.1.9)

Figure 3.2   ISO 27001/2-based ISPF—example. ISO 27001/2 security clauses and controls, as documented in ISO 27001/2:2013, can be allocated to the four information security policy levels into 28 policies. The policy titles and associated ISO 27001/2 security clauses and controls are listed to the right.

policy for each control family. Even though the FISMA controls are grouped according to the control family, this grouping is not the most logical grouping of controls when it comes to organizing an information security policy set. Using the 4 levels of security policies described in Figure 3.2, FISMA security controls can be allocated amongst 17 policies shown in Figure 3.1 at these 4 policy levels.

3.3.1.2 Benefits of the FISMA Security Controls Framework   The benefits of using a FISMA-based security controls framework for the creation of an ISPF include industry acceptance, use of supplemental guidance, and the wide availability of crosswalks and mappings to other associated information security regulations.

- *Industry accepted standard.* The FISMA framework has a well-established acceptance within the IT and security community. If ever challenged on your choice of a framework pointing to the one produced by the NIST goes a long way.
- *Supplemental guidance.* Within the NIST SP 800-53 document is supplemental guidance to explain and provide rationale for almost all of the controls. Furthermore, NIST has produced an extensive catalog of Special Publications (800 series) providing supporting guidance on many information security and privacy topics.
- *Availability of crosswalks.* Many available maps from the FISMA framework to other information security regulations exist within the NIST SP 800-53 document itself, within other information security regulations (e.g., IRS Publication 1075), or as separate documents (e.g., NIST SP 800-64 maps 800-53 to the HIPAA Security Rule).

3.3.2 ISO 27001:2013 Framework

An information security standard created by the International Standards Organization (ISO) and the International Electrotechnical Commission (IEC) has the long title: "Information Technology—Security Techniques—Information Security Management Systems—Requirements" but is commonly known as ISO 27001. The standard is a specification for an information security management system (ISMS). An ISMS is an organizational set of policies, procedures, and processes that set forth the requirements and process for implementing a set of physical, administrative, and technical controls to protect organizational information assets. The ISO 27001 was first developed in 2005 and its most recent edition is 2013. The standard is based on an effort that started in 1995 with the British Standard (BS7799-1 and BS7799-2) and later BS17799-1 and BS17799-2.

The ISO 27001/2 framework is clearly aligned with an ISPF. Using ISO 27001/2 as a framework for the development of information security policies can be rather straightforward, but first the structure of the ISO 27001 must be interpreted. The ISO 27001 has seven clauses and a reference to 114 controls in 14 groups. The clauses are required but rather high level. The clauses (4-10) of ISO 27001 are listed in 5: ISO 27001 clauses, 4 along with the associated ISPF. Policies, procedures, and processes aligning to these clauses will be rather high level (or programmatic) as well. For example, Clause 6.1.2 requires that the organization "define and apply an information security risk assessment process." An information security risk assessment process documents the minimum requirements for a risk assessment, the output of risk assessments, and the workflow of the results. Guidance for the development of an information security risk assess process is presented below:

Security Risk Assessment Process Guidance: The following guidance is provided for the performance of information security risk assessments. This guidance is presented within the context of the phases of an information security risk assessment process. Namely, the preparation, the performance, and the communication of the results for an information security risk assessment.

- *Information Security Risk Assessment Preparation.* Preparation for an information security risk assessment helps to ensure that the department derives the most value from this exercise and establishes the context of the risk management process. The departments shall consider the following steps in preparing for an information security risk assessment.
  a. *Identify Purpose.* The obvious purpose for an information security risk assessment is to provide information to the system owners regarding the risk to sensitive data and critical information systems so that they may make appropriate decisions regarding how to address those risks. However, information security risk assessments are also required periodically based on applicable regulations, provide oversight to the security operations of the system, or could be the direct (and required) action from a recent audit or inspection. It is important that the department clearly understands and identifies the purpose of the information security risk assessment and conveys

that to the team performing and overseeing the assessment in order to ensure project success.

b. *Define Assessment Boundaries.* An information security risk assessment shall be limited to defined physical and logical boundaries. A physical boundary identifies the physical limit of the assessment such as network components (e.g., workstations, servers, routers, switches), security components (e.g., IDS, firewalls), network media (e.g., cabling), peripherals, buildings, and rooms. A logical boundary identifies the logical limit of the assessment such as the functions of the system, services provided, applications, and network segments.

c. *Define Level of Rigor.* An information security risk assessment shall have a defined level of rigor specifying the depth of analysis to be performed. The level of rigor may be specified by hours (or other resource metrics) to be expended, or by listing the methods of data gathering.

d. *Document Scope Limitations and Constraints.* An information security risk assessment is generally expected to cover all relevant administrative, technical, and physical controls. When the scope is limited or constraints are placed on the task of assessing the risk to the state information system the budget unit needs to ensure that these constraints are reasonable. If a budget unit chooses to limit the scope of the risk assessment (e.g., physical security controls are out of scope) then there should be some rationale provided on why such a limitation is reasonable (e.g., physical security controls are reviewed under another assessment program).

e. *Document Risk Model.* There are a variety of reasonable security risk models that may be used in the performance of an information security risk assessment (e.g., NIST 800-30). The budget unit (or the contractor for the budget unit) may use any reasonable security risk model provided the model accounts for the following aspects of a baseline information security risk assessment.

f. *Document Risk Elements.* The information security risk model shall identify and document the elements to be reviewed, assessed, and analyzed in order to determine the risk to the state information system. These elements typically include: threats, assets, vulnerabilities, likelihood, and impact.

g. *Document Risk Calculation.* The information security risk model shall identify the process by which risk is determined. This is typically in the form of a risk calculation, estimate based on parameters, or a risk determination table based on the risk elements listed above.

- *Information Security Risk Assessment Performance.* The effective performance of an information security risk assessment is critical to the accuracy and usefulness of the assessment. The departments shall consider the following steps in the performance of an information security risk assessment.

a. *Objectivity.* Consistent with requirement 6.5.1.1 of P8120 (Information Security Program Policy), an information security risk assessment shall be performed by impartial assessors or assessment teams. Impartiality requires that the assessment team have no conflict of interest between the development, selection, and/or operation of the security controls under assessment.

b. *Adequate Data Gathering.* An information security risk assessment shall have adequate data gathered on the controls within the physical and logical boundaries of the assessment. Adequacy of the data gathering is largely subjective but the departments shall be hesitant to rely on information security risk assessments that have too few data points to draw an accurate conclusion or assessments that rely on interviews of surveys alone from those in charge of the assessed controls. To the extent possible the department should ensure that effective data-gathering approaches from reviewing documents, interviewing personnel, observing behavior, inspecting controls, and testing controls are utilized.

c. *Defendable Analysis.* An information security risk assessment shall include a documented and defendable analysis of the data gathered to support findings. Information security risk assessments typically provide such analysis in the form of tables or charts. Each finding/recommendation shall be traceable to sufficient evidence of the vulnerability that is being addressed.

- *Information Security Risk Assessment Documentation.* The effective and accurate communication of results from an information security risk assessment is critical to the usefulness of the assessment. The departments shall consider the following steps in the documentation of an information security risk assessment.

a. *Communication with Key Staff.* The results of an information security risk assessment provide pertinent information and guidance to system owners, information security officers, and chief information officers within the budget unit. The results of the assessment shall be shared with budget unit director, CIO, information security officer, and system owners at a minimum. The state CISO may also be included in the dissemination of the assessment results.

b. *Communication with Custodians and Others.* The results of the information security risk assessment include recommendations for improvements (e.g., patch information systems, develop procedures, implement additional controls) that will need to be conveyed to those in charge of implementing these changes. When relevant, all available evidence of the associated vulnerabilities and details of the recommended solutions shall be made available to the system custodians, staff members, or contractors tasked with confirming the vulnerability and/or implementing the recommended solution. Keep in mind that the principle of least privilege shall be applied here and there and some details may be deemed irrelevant and sensitive and therefore not conveyed to others.

c. *Clear Recommendations.* An information security risk assessment shall provide a report with clear recommendations that identify the control gap or risk and the recommended solution or solution set to address the control gap or risk. The departments may want to require that the information security risk assessment recommendations provide information on the cost of the recommendation as well.

In addition to the seven clauses, Annex A contains a set of controls that provide additional structure for an information security policy set.* The controls (Annex A) of ISO 27001, along with their associated ISPF, are listed in Table 3.3.

3.3.2.1 Using the ISO 27001/2 Framework as a Policy Framework   Some of the ISO 27001/2 clauses and controls are high-level requirements that describe IT program requirements or processes, whereas others are lower-level requirements more suited for system control requirements or even standards. Using the four levels of security policies described in Table 3.4, controls can be allocated among 28 policies at these levels.

---

* Clause 6.1.3 requires a risk treatment process in which the organization determines appropriate controls based on a risk treatment process. It is this clause (6.1.3) that references the 114 controls in Annex A of ISO 27001. For the purpose of defining an ISO 27001 information security policy framework, both the clauses (4–10) and the controls (Annex A) will be referenced.

Table 3.3 ISO 27001 Annex A Policy and Procedure Controls

NO.	ISO 27001 CONTROL	DESCRIPTION	FRAMEWORK POLICY
A.5	Information security policies	Information security program requirements	• Information security policy set [A.5.1.1] "policies"
A6	Information security organization	Information security management framework	• Information security responsibilities [A.6.1.1] "defined" • Mobile device security policy [A.6.2.1] "policy" • Telework security policy [A.6.2.2] "policy"
A7	Human resource security	Information security responsibilities	• Employee and contractor security responsibility agreements [A.7.1.1] "agreements" • Disciplinary process [A.7.2.3] "formal … process" • (Include in disciplinary process) Termination process [A.7.3.1] "defined"
A8	Asset management	Define asset protection requirements	• Asset inventory [A.8.1.1] "identified … drawn up" • Acceptable use of assets [A.8.1.3] "documented" • Classification labeling procedures [A.8.2.2] "procedures … developed" • Asset handling procedures [A.8.2.3] "procedures … developed" • Removable media management procedures [A.8.3.1] "procedures … implemented" • Media disposal procedures [A.8.3.2] "formal procedures"
A9	Access control	Access control requirements and processes	• Access control policy [A.9.1.1] "policy … documented" • Account management process • User registration process [A.9.2.1] "formal … process … implemented" • User access provisioning process [A.9.2.2] "formal … process … implemented" • Authentication information management process [A.9.2.4] "formal management process" • Secure login procedure [A.9.4.2] "procedure"

(Continued)

Table 3.3 (*Continued*) ISO 27001 Annex A Policy and Procedure Controls

NO.	ISO 27001 CONTROL	DESCRIPTION	FRAMEWORK POLICY
A10	Cryptography	Effective use of cryptography to secure assets	• Cryptographic controls policy [A.10.1.1] "policy … developed" • Key management policy [A.10.1.2] "policy … "

A11	Physical security	Effective use of physical controls to secure assets	• Physical security plan
			  • Physical security perimeter diagrams [A.11.1.1] "defined"
			  • Physical office security designs [A.11.1.3] "designed"
			  • Natural disaster protection designs [A.11.1.4] "designed"
			  • Secure working area procedures [A.11.1.5] "procedures … designed"
			  • Clear desk policy [A.11.2.9] "policy … adopted"

A12	Operations security	Secure operations of information processing	• Operating procedures [A.12.1.1] "procedures … documented" • Backup policy [A.12.3.1] "backup policy" • Software installation procedures [A.12.5.1] "procedures … implemented" • User software installation rules [A.12.6.2] "rules … established and implemented" • System audit policy [A.12.7.1] "requirements … planned and agreed"
A13	Communications security	Secure networks	• Network service security requirements [A.13.1.2] "requirements … identified … included in agreements" • Information transfer policy and procedures [A.13.2.2] "formal … policies, procedures" • Secure transfer agreements [A.13.2.2] "agreements" • Nondisclosure agreements [A.13.2.4] "requirements … identified … and documented"
A14	System acquisition, development, and maintenance	Secure lifecycle development	• Information security requirements specification [A.14.1.1] "requirements" • Secure coding rules [A.14.2.1] "rules … established" • Change control procedures [A.14.2.2] "formal change control procedures" • Secure system engineering principles [A.14.2.5] "principles … established" • System acceptance testing program and criteria [A.14.2.9] "program … criteria … established"

(Continued)

Table 3.3 (*Continued*)   ISO 27001 Annex A Policy and Procedure Controls

NO.	ISO 27001 CONTROL	DESCRIPTION	FRAMEWORK POLICY
A15	Supplier relationship	Protect assets from suppliers	• Supplier information security requirements [A.15.1.1] "requirements … documented"
A16	Information security incident management	Effective management of security incidents	• Incident management responsibilities [A.16.1.1] "responsibilities …. established" • Incident management procedures [A.16.1.1] "procedures …. established" • Evidence collection procedures [A.16.1.7] "define … procedures"
A17	Business continuity management	Effectively management business continuity	• Business continuity requirements [A.17.1.1] "determine …. requirements" • Business continuity processes and procedures [A.17.1.2] "establish document … processes, procedures"
A18	Compliance	Ensure effective compliance with applicable security requirements	• Applicable regulations and requirements [A.18.1.1] "requirements … explicitly identified, documented" • Compliance procedures [A.18.1.2] "procedures …. implemented"

Note: The ISO 27001 requires that an organization's ISMS implement a risk assessment to determine appropriate controls. Annex A of ISO 27001 offers a set of 114 controls many of which are controls for security policies or procedures.

Table 3.4 ISO 27001 Clauses

NO.	CLAUSE/CONTROL	DESCRIPTION	FRAMEWORK POLICY
4	Organizational context	• External and internal issues • Stakeholder needs • ISMS scope • ISMS	• ISMS (introduction) • Stakeholders • Relevant criteria, regulations, and requirements • Scope, boundaries, applicable information systems, and organizational units
5	Leadership	• Top management support • Information security policy • Organizational roles and responsibilities	• Statement of senior management commitment (include in ISMS) • Security policy[a] • Information security roles and responsibilities

6	Planning	• Information security risk management
		  • Information security risk assessment
		  • Information security risk treatment[b]
		• Information security plan
			• Information security plan
			  • Information security risk management process (risk assessment, risk management, and risk treatment)
			• Information security objectives

7	Support	• Ensure adequate and competent staff
		
		• Security awareness training
		• ISMS communication plan
		• Document, update, distribute, and protect ISMS documents
			• Personnel security plan
			  • Resource plan
			  • Job descriptions
			  • Competence documentation (education, training, and experience)
			• Security awareness program
			• Communication plan
			• Document control plan
			  • Protection, distribution, storage, control, and retention

(Continued)

Table 3.4 (*Continued*) ISO 27001 Clauses

NO.	CLAUSE/CONTROL	DESCRIPTION	FRAMEWORK POLICY
8	Operation	• Implementation of information security plans[c]	• No additional documents

9	Performance evaluation	• ISMS performance monitoring	• Information security program monitoring plan
			  • Monitoring plan (who, what, when)
			  • Metrics for security controls and processes

		• Internal audit	• Internal audit plan • Frequency, methods, responsibilities, planning, and reporting

		• Management review	• ISMS management review
			  • Review intervals, status, changes in issues
			  • Document decisions and evidence

10	Improvement	• Corrective action • Continuous improvement	• (Include in ISMS management review) Document nonconformities, corrective actions, and results of corrective actions

Note: The ISO 27001 requires that an organization's ISMS implement the seven clauses. Following the organization of the ISO clauses (together with the requirements in Table 3.5) provides an outline for an ISPF.

[a] An "information security policy" is a policy that dictates the requirements of the information security policies such as coverage, dissemination, and maintenance.

[b] Again, clause 6.1.3 (information security risk treatment) references Annex A and the selection of appropriate controls. It is the selected controls that provide the balance of the structure for the security controls framework.

[c] The operation clause is really just the implementation of the planning clause. For the purposes of creating an ISPF, this clause may be addressed in the same policies as those that address clause 6.

An example of an ISO 27001/2-based information security policy set is illustrated in Figure 3.2. This is only an example, as ISO 27001/2 does not specify a policy framework.

3.3.2.2 Benefits of the ISO 27001/2 Security Controls Framework   The benefits of using a ISO 27001/2-based security controls framework for the creation of an ISPF include industry acceptance, use of supplemental guidance provided by the ISO, wide availability of crosswalks and mappings to other associated IT, and security regulations.

- *Industry accepted standard.* The ISO/IEC 27001 standard is quite literally an international standard. While not a required standard for any specific industry—like NIST 800-53 for US Federal Government or the COBIT standard for publicly traded companies—the ISO/IEC 27001 standard is well known and used internationally.
- *Supplemental guidance.* The ISO provides some implementation guidance and a great deal of training, guidance, and assistance is available from commercial groups.
- *Availability of crosswalks.* Many available maps from the ISO/IEC 27001 framework to other related frameworks and regulations are available from ISO/IEC, NIST, US-CERT, and other groups. These include mappings from ISO/IEC 27001 to NIST 800-53, COBIT, HIPAA, PCI DSS, and others.

3.3.3 COBIT Framework

COBIT is an IT management and governance controls framework created by the Information Systems Audit and Control Association (ISACA). This framework has been around since 1996 and most recently updated to COBIT version 5 in 2012. While the COBIT framework is primarily used to establish and manage an IT and governance controls framework, the basic structure of the framework also provides the basis of an ISPF.

The IT management and governance controls within the COBIT framework are organized into four domains: plan and organize, acquire and implement, deliver and support, and monitor and evaluate. The COBIT framework contains 34 processes allocated across the four domains. The domains and processes of COBIT are listed in Table 3.5.

Table 3.5 COBIT Domains and Processes

COBIT DOMAIN	COBIT PROCESS
Plan and organize	• PO1 Define a strategic plan
	• PO2 Define the information architecture
	• PO3 Determine technological direction
	• PO4 Define the IT processes, organization, and relationships
	• PO5 Manage the IT investment
	• PO6 Communicate management aims and direction
	• PO7 Manage IT human resources
	• PO8 Manage quality
	• PO9 Assess and manage IT risks
	• PO10 Manage projects
Acquire and implement	• AI1 Identify automated solutions
	• AI2 Acquire and maintain application software
	• AI3 Acquire and maintain technology infrastructure
	• AI4 Enable operation and use
	• AI5 Procure IT resources
	• AI6 Manage changes
	• AI7 Install and accredit solutions and changes
Deliver and support	• DS1 Define and manage service levels
	• DS2 Manage third-party services
	• DS3 Manage performance and capacity
	• DS4 Ensure continuous service
	• DS5 Ensure information systems security
	• DS6 Identify and allocate costs
	• DS7 Educate and train users
	• DS8 Manage service desk and incidents
	• DS9 Manage the configuration
	• DS10 Manage problems
	• DS11 Manage data
	• DS12 Manage physical environment
	• DS13 Manage operations
Monitor and evaluate	• ME1 Monitor and evaluate IT performance
	• ME2 Monitor and evaluate internal control
	• ME3 Ensure compliance with external requirements
	• ME4 Provide IT governance

Note: The IT management and governance controls listed in COBIT are organized into four domains and identified with a domain digraph and process number.

Within each domain is a set of process requirements designed to meet the business objectives of the organization. Each process requirement is sequentially numbered within the domain (e.g., PO1, PO2). Each of these processes can have one or more control objectives associated with them (e.g., PO1.1, PO1.2). These control objectives are in turn met by a set of controls. For example, the domain of "Plan and Organize" (PO) has the associated process "PO2: Define the Information Architecture." The PO2 process has several associated control objectives including "PO2.e: Data Classification Scheme." The PO2.3 control objective is met through six controls defining the creation of a data classification scheme, definition of classification levels, identification of business owners, the classification of data within the scheme, responsibility education, and labeling of data and media.

3.3.3.1 Using the COBIT Framework as a Policy Framework   Some of the COBIT requirements are high-level requirements that describe IT program requirements, whereas others are lower-level requirements more suited for system control requirements or even standards. Using the four levels of security policies described in Figure 3.3, COBIT controls can be allocated among 17 policies at these four policy levels.

An example of a COBIT-based information security policy set is illustrated in Figure 3.3. This is only an example as COBIT does not specify a policy framework. Also, COBIT is more focused on IT controls than information security in general, but this is a COBIT-based policy framework in that it maps to the COBIT control practices and objectives to a set of information security requirements.

3.3.3.2 Benefits of the COBIT Security Controls Framework   The benefits of using a COBIT-based security controls framework for the creation of an ISPF include industry acceptance, use of supplemental guidance provided by the ISACA and the IT Governance Institute, and the wide availability of crosswalks and mappings to other associated IT and security regulations.

- *Industry accepted standard.* The COBIT framework has a well-established acceptance within the IT and audit community. If ever challenged on your choice of a framework pointing

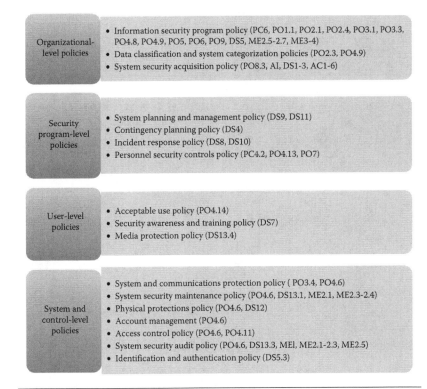

Figure 3.3   COBIT-based ISPF—example. COBIT security controls, as documented in COBIT control practices (v4.0), can be allocated to the four information security policy levels into 17 policies. The policy titles and associated COBIT control practices, or control objectives, are listed to the right.

to the one preferred by your auditor goes a long way. This is especially true within public companies required to have their internal controls for financial information systems reviewed (e.g., Sarbanes-Oxley [SOX] requirements).

- *Supplemental guidance.* Both ISACA and the IT Governance Institute provide a wide variety of implementation guides regarding the interpretation and application of the COBIT control practices and objectives.
- *Availability of crosswalks.* Many crosswalks are available that map the COBIT framework objectives and controls to other related frameworks. These include mappings from COBIT to the ISO 27001, The Software Engineering Institute's Capability Maturity Model, and the Information Technology Infrastructure Library (ITIL).

3.3.4 HMG ISPF Framework

Her Majesty's Government (HMG) Security Policy Framework (SPF) was issued April 2014 and set out the expectations of how HMG organizations and others shall handle sensitive data and apply appropriate security controls. These expectations are enumerated in terms of "security outcomes," which describe the desired consequences from the security controls put in place by the organization. The nine security outcomes are briefly described in Table 3.6.

The HMG ISPF does not specify processes or controls but instead the security outcomes above as guidance. Each organization is expected to consider its own mission and risk environments in selecting proper controls.

3.3.4.1 Using the HMG ISPF as a Policy Framework   Some of the HMG ISPF security outcomes are high-level outcomes that describe security program requirements, whereas others are lower-level requirements more suited as guidance for system control requirements or even standards. Using the four levels of security policies described in Table 3.6 can be allocated among eight policies at these four policy levels.

An example of a HMG ISPF-based information security policy set is illustrated in Figure 3.4. This is only an example as HMG ISPF lists security outcomes that "do not specify particular processes" or a specific policy framework.

3.3.4.2 Benefits of the HMG ISPF   The benefits of using the HMG ISPF for the creation of an information ISPF include government acceptance and simplicity of design.

- *Government accepted standard.* The HMG ISPF is mandatory for HMG organizations.
- *Simplicity of design.* The HMG ISPF results in a recommended eight policies (in our example). This simplistic design is useful for those organizations that prefer a more minimal ISPF and approachable design.

3.4 Tailoring Information SPFs

An information ISPF provides a general structure for organizing policy statements into a complete and coherent policy structure.

Table 3.6 HMG ISPF Outcomes

HMG ISPF SECURITY OUTCOME	DESCRIPTION
Security organization	Organizations shall ensure an appropriate security governance structure including a senior information risk owner, a departmental security officer, an information asset owner(s), information risk assessment and management specialists, board-level oversight, and oversight of service providers and other trusted third parties.
Culture and awareness	Organizations shall establish a security culture aligned with the organization's risk and a security training program backed by processes and incentives along with continuous improvement to ensure best practices.
Risk management	Organizations shall assess security risk to enable informed business decisions. This includes a set of security policies and procedures that support risk management; an understanding of organizational security risks; methods and trained personnel to assess threats, vulnerabilities and impacts; the implementation of controls to mitigate risk; and an assurance process to monitor and manage risk.
Information	Organizations shall ensure staff are well trained to handle sensitive information appropriately, establish mechanisms to classify and protect information, and ensure adequate controls are in place to protect sensitive information.
Technology and services	Organizations shall identify any technology or services that are part of the critical infrastructure and appropriately manage risk. Security controls shall be selected and implemented based on a risk-based process. The controls shall be kept current, managed, protect against malicious behavior, and ensure the technology is resistant to disruption.
Personnel security	Organizations shall implement security policies and processes that include background checks, an insider threat program, and a program to drive the security culture.
Physical security	Organizations shall implement appropriate physical security measures that protect the working environment. These measures shall include building design process and plans, the implementation of defense in-depth design to protect against unauthorized access, and substantial controls for physical sites housing critical infrastructure.
Security incident response	Organizations shall implement policies and procedures to appropriately handle security incidents and reduce damage to sensitive assets and critical information systems. These policies and procedures shall cover business arrangements to maintain key business services, the method for risk and vulnerability assessments, plans to be followed in the event of specific threats, management structures enacted during incidents and disasters, and reporting mechanisms to appropriate parties.
Security risk management overview	Organizations shall meet the security outcomes described above and annually report their compliance.

Note: The outcomes listed in HMG ISPF are organized into nine areas.

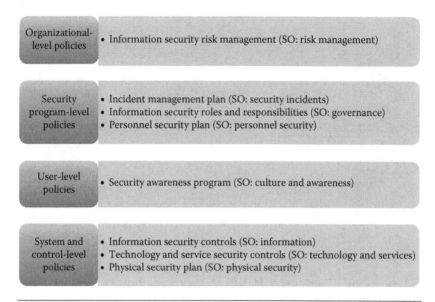

Figure 3.4   HMG ISPF—example. The HMG ISPF can be allocated to the four information security policy levels into eight policies. The policy titles and associated security outcomes are listed to the right.

However, just as information security policies themselves are not a one-size-fits-all document, neither is the information ISPF. In an effort to address all business needs, information SPFs will often be tailored for the specific organization it serves.

3.4.1 Customer and Business Requirements

The organization may have several unique business requirements that drive the development of additional information security controls or even additional information security policies thus affecting the base framework. It is important to start with the framework but to be flexible enough to accommodate business needs when developing a platform upon which to build policies for an organization. For example, a pharmaceutical company may recognize extreme asset values in a building within which it works on new products. With these extreme asset values come additional risks such as industrial espionage and a need for the implementation of additional physical security controls not present in other organizations. In the case that these controls are unique to some environments (e.g., data centers, research, and development facilities), there may be a need to have an additional physical security controls policy for very sensitive areas.

3.4.2 *Importance of Completeness*

Even the most frequently cited or used information security frameworks have notable gaps in terms of information security controls. For example, the FISMA framework (based on NIST SP 800-53 controls) is not very specific when it comes to measurable elements of a security program (e.g., testing, validation, and assessment specifics). On the other hand, the ISO 27001 framework does not provide many specific requirements in the area of network security (e.g., firewall architecture and settings, wireless access point isolation, and secure domain name system [DNS]). In both cases, the standard is used as a general framework and the organization should review its own security needs and tailor the framework as needed to suit its business needs (e.g., expand the framework to include additional policies, topics, requirements, or specific values).

3.4.3 *Adding and Mapping Regulations*

Organizations will also need to tailor the information ISPF for their own use according to the need to accommodate and map information security regulations, standards, and requirements. These policy additions stem from customer requests, industry regulations, and other business-driven requirements. For each of the required information security requirement documents (e.g., HIPAA, PCI DSS, and North American Electric Reliability Corporation Critical Infrastructure Protection Standards), the organization should (a) ensure all requirements are documented in the standard policy set and (b) create a crosswalk that supports compliance reviews.

- *Ensure all requirements are documented.* There must be an accounting for each and every requirement in an information security regulation or standard that the organization seeks to implement. In many cases, the information security framework will already have a populated information security control that meets the document requirement. For example, PCI DSS requires basic security awareness training and this requirement is already accounted for in the FISMA framework. In other cases, an information security control required in a regulation or standard may not be currently populated in the framework. For example, PCI DSS requires that vulnerability scans be performed by a qualified vulnerability scanning vendor who is free from conflict of interest. Such a requirement does not exist in the FISMA framework but it can be easily added under the vulnerability scanning section of the FISMA framework.

- *Compliance crosswalk.* While developing and revising the information ISPF, it may help to track the regulation or standard requirements and where they are addressed in the tailored framework and resulting set of policies. There are several approaches to tracking this mapping such as adding references to the original standards at the end of each policy statement or creating a crosswalk matrix based on the regulation that maps each regulation statement to a specific policy statement. The creation of a compliance crosswalk may be tedious work but in order to ensure the completeness of the policy set it must be performed. As a side benefit, once completed, the compliance crosswalks support compliance reviews of the specific standard or regulation.

3.5 Deriving a Policy Set from a Framework

An information security policy set is the determination of the number of policies, topics, titles, and audiences for your organization's policies that map to the information ISPF. Figure 3.4 provides good examples of how to derive the information security policy set from a given information ISPF. Prior to beginning the process of writing individual information security policy statements, it is important to lock down the definition of the information security policy set. Specifically, the following elements should be considered:

- *Number of policies.* There is no set rule here. Some organizations tend to modify policies often and end up with many (e.g., dozens or even hundreds of policies). Organizations with many policies typically have a very good support and search structure of online policies so that stakeholders have ready access and are able to find what they need quickly when attempting to comply with organizational policies. Other organizations opt for fewer policies. Typically, these organizations group their policies according to the audience (e.g., one policy for all users and one policy for all administrators) or by audience and topic (Figure 3.4 supports this number of policies). It is important to understand the organizational preference for the number of policies while the policy set is being derived from the framework.

- *Audience.* Regardless of the number of policies created, it is highly advised that each policy be limited to a specific audience (e.g., all users). Many policies may contain sensitive information (e.g., patch system vulnerabilities within 7 days) that should be limited on a need-to-know basis. In addition, policies with a defined audience can be written to the intended audience with an understanding of familiar terms and knowledge of the audience.

- *Topics.* When outlining the information security policy set from the information ISPF, it is important to create a list of topics to be covered. For example, if you have identified an information security program policy, then you can start identifying requirement areas that would be covered in an information security management program such as System Security Planning, System Security Policies, Security Risk Management, Information Security Program Management, and Security Assessments and Authorizations.

- *Titles.* The title of each information security policy should reflect the topics covered within. You may start with working titles to assist in determining the general nature of the policy (e.g., secure hiring practices) and then revise the title when the allocation of requirements to policies is complete. In many cases, the working title may need to be expanded to cover additional requirements allocated to the policy (e.g., personnel security protections).

EXERCISES

What are the major benefits of using an information ISPF to guide the development of information security policies?

1. If your organization utilizes ITIL, would you consider the ITIL framework as a reasonable framework for the development of information security policies? Why or why not?

2. Using your own organizational set of security policies (or a set your instructor provides) identify the ISPF used.
   a. Is the framework easily identifiable and consistently used in the creation of policies and procedures?
   b. Is the policy set complete? If not what major policy elements, topics, or controls are missing?
   c. If you were to add a policy statement regarding the use of intrusion detections information systems and the placement of sensors, what policy would you modify? Or would you create a new one?
   d. Write one or more policy statements covering the use of intrusion detection information systems, the placement of their sensors, and the review of their logs or alerts.

3. Using the same organizational policy set used in question 1,
   a. Provide an estimate of how many hours it would take to update the policy set to meet a revised standard such as PCI DSS.
   b. Provide an estimate on how many hours it would take to review the policy for compliance with a standard such as PCI DSS.

4

INFORMATION SECURITY POLICY DETAILS

Once an information security policy framework has been established and the decision to develop a new policy (or revise an existing one) is complete, the details of policy development can be addressed. For the purposes of a more complete and clear explanation, it is assumed that new policies will be developed rather than revising existing policies. For policy projects involving the revision of existing policies, the instructions and guidance presented here should be easily transferable to a policy revision project.

Information security policies represent the expectations of senior management as to how the overall security program, system controls, and user behavior should be implemented. These policies are of the highest level of the information security policy framework. Information security policies are typically strictly formatted and well structured to accommodate the required document elements (e.g., authority, scope, and references) and to accommodate senior management review. There is no room for fluff (e.g., long explanations or reasons for policy requirements)—just stick to the requirements in these documents. Long discussions or explanations of why certain requirements are being enacted detract from directness of senior management requirements and reduce the clarity of what is required versus what is a good idea.

There is a lot of variation from organization to organization in terms of the format of an information security policy. How the information is organized, ordered, or formatted should follow any existing organizational templates for documents that must be approved by senior management. For the sake of illustration and example, the following format is suggested. Again, it is not required that an information security policy be organized precisely like this example, but most of these sections should be covered in your own organization's template.

4.1 Front Matter

Like many organizational documents that must be approved by senior management, the information security policy should conform to organizational standards. Most organizations have a standard template for policies (Table 4.1). Information security policies should follow the organizational template. These templates will include the standard header and footer, document-style elements (e.g., font, text size, and indents), and most likely the following sections for policies and procedures.

Table 4.1   Security Policy Template Front Matter

POLICY TEMPLATE SECTION	DESCRIPTION
Authority	This section specifies the laws, regulations, and/or executive management with the authority to require policy statements in the policy topic area.
Purpose	This section describes the purpose of the policy. This is also referred to as the "topic sentence" in general writing but for policy documents, it is easier to just call it the purpose. Typically, the purpose is to establish a set of minimum security controls for information systems within the organization.
Scope	This section describes reach of the policy in terms of who and what information systems are affected by it. Scope statements typically cover application to departments, personnel, information systems, data, and devices.
Roles and responsibilities	This section lists the various roles involved with the policy and policy enforcement and each of their responsibilities for implementing, adhering to, or enforcing the policy statements. Within the information security policy set, the same titles and roles should be used throughout eliminating confusion. Standard roles include information security officer, information security manager, system owner, data owner, system custodian, and user.
Definitions	This section provides a set of terms that may require definitions to ensure there is no confusion or ambiguity in the policies. Organizations should take care to ensure a consistent set of standard definitions throughout all policies.
Revision history	This section keeps track of revisions to the document. Revision history should include a date, revision number, and a brief description of the changes.

Note: Most organizations have standard templates for the development of policies and procedures. These templates typically address standard document elements in the front part of the document (e.g., "front matter"). The organization's standard template should be used in the creation of information security policy and procedures.

An example of a policy and procedure template is provided below:

POLICY 8###: [POLICY NAME]

DOCUMENT NUMBER	P8###
Effective date	Draft
Revision	1.0

AUTHORITY

To effectuate the mission and purposes of the ACME organization, the department shall establish a coordinated plan and program for information technology (IT) implemented and maintained through policies, standards, and procedures (PSPs) as authorized by the Information Security Department Charter (P8000, September 1, 2015).

PURPOSE

The purpose of this policy is to establish the baseline controls for the protection of ACME information systems and their communications.

SCOPE

Application to departments. This policy shall apply to all departments of the ACME organization.

Application to information systems. This policy shall apply to all ACME information systems:

(P)—Policy statements preceded by "(P)" are required for organization information systems categorized as protected.

(P-PCI)—Policy statements preceded by "(P-PCI)" are required for organization information systems with payment card industry data (e.g., cardholder data).

(P-PHI)—Policy statements preceded by "(P-PHI)" are required for organization information systems with protected health-care information.

(P-FTI)—Policy statements preceded by "(P-FTI)" are required for organization information systems with federal taxpayer information.

Information owned or under the control of the U.S. Government shall comply with the federal classification authority and federal protection requirements.

EXCEPTIONS

PSPs may be expanded or exceptions may be taken by following the ACME policy exception procedure.

Existing IT products and services. Department subject matter experts (SMEs) should enquire with the vendor and the procurement office to ascertain whether the contract provides for additional products or services to attain compliance with PSPs prior to submitting a request for an exception in accordance with the ACME policy exception procedure.

IT products and services procurement. Prior to selecting and procuring IT products and services, department SMEs shall consider IT PSPs when specifying, scoping, and evaluating solutions to meet current and planned requirements.

[Department Name] has taken the following exceptions to the ACME policy framework:

SECTION NUMBER	EXCEPTION	EXPLANATION/BASIS

ROLES AND RESPONSIBILITIES

ACME chief information officer (CIO) shall

- Be ultimately responsible for the correct and thorough completion of IT PSPs throughout all ACME departments.

Chief information security officer (CISO) shall

- Advise the CIO on the completeness and adequacy of the department activities and documentation provided to ensure compliance with ACME IT PSPs throughout all departments.
- Review and approve department security and privacy PSPs and requested exceptions from the ACME security and privacy PSPs.
- Identify and convey to the CIO the risk to ACME information systems and data based on the current implementation of security controls and mitigation options to improve security.

Department head shall

- Be responsible for the correct and thorough completion of department IT PSPs within his or her department.
- Ensure department compliance with system and communication protections policy.
- Promote efforts within the department to establish and maintain the effective use of ACME information systems and assets.

Department IT lead shall

- Work with the department head to ensure the correct and thorough completion of department IT PSPs within the department.
- Ensure this policy is periodically reviewed and updated to reflect changes in requirements.

Department information security lead shall

- Advise the department IT lead on the completeness and adequacy of the department activities and documentation provided to ensure compliance with department IT PSPs.
- Ensure the development and implementation of adequate controls enforcing this policy for the department.
- Ensure that all personnel understand their responsibilities with respect to the protection of ACME information systems and their communications.

Supervisors of ACME employees and contractors shall

- Ensure users are appropriately trained and educated on this policy.
- Monitor employee activities to ensure compliance.

System users of ACME information systems shall

- Become familiar with this policy and related PSPs.
- Adhere to PSPs regarding the scope of this policy.

4.2 Policy Statements

The policy statement is the core of the policy document. It is the policy statement that provides the direction, requirement, or order for the minimal security controls of information systems of behaviors of people. Therefore, it is important to state the policy statement in clear and concise language. In the examples below, the policy statements use straightforward language—do not use ambiguous or technical terms to describe what is required.

> ### POLICY STATEMENT EXAMPLE: ACCEPTABLE USE STATEMENT
>
> *Computer tampering*: Unauthorized access, interception, modification, or destruction of any computer, computer system, ACME information system, computer programs, or data shall be prohibited.

> ### POLICY STATEMENT EXAMPLE: ACCOUNT MANAGEMENT STATEMENT
>
> *Account approval*: The department shall require documented approvals by authorized staff for requests to create, modify, and enable ACME information system accounts.

To create policy statements that are clear and concise, consider the following elements of the policy statement:

- *Subject.* This is the "who" of the policy statement and directs the behavior of a person or role. In general, it is better to identify the role instead of the person (by name) in a policy statement as people move in and out of roles and would therefore require more frequent policy updates. In cases in which the subject is a system, system component, or technology, it directs the technical or physical requirements of the device.
- *Terms: Shall, should, and will.* Information security policies are a collection of requirements for the organization, organizational roles, and information systems. Policy statements, as the embodiment of these requirements, need to use mandatory terms. Although many terms have been used throughout information security policies in the industry, it is strongly recommended that the use of terms be limited to a defined and clear set used consistently throughout the document. The following terms are recommended:
  - *Shall*: This term is used to indicate a requirement, meaning that it must be implemented. Statements that use the term "shall" are mandatory requirements, and verifiable in a contractual relationship. In many circles (including the ISO community), statements without the word "shall" are not requirements.
  - *Will*: This term is used to indicate a statement of fact or that will be true in the future. Statements that use the term "will" are not verifiable in a contract as they are simply a statement of fact (i.e., it is already happening). Limit the use of this term to conditions that are already in place. For example, if a background check is currently run for all employees, it is acceptable to use the statement: "Background checks will be performed on all employees as part of the screening process." Be aware that the use of the term "will" does not indicate a requirement and is therefore not verifiable in a contractual relationship.
  - *Should*: This term is used to indicate a nonmandatory goal that is to be addressed but not formally verified. In general, policy statements would not contain the term "should" because it is not a requirement. However, sometimes, there

are important issues that are not verifiable that you still want to convey to the audience. For example, requiring the application of system-engineering principles throughout the life cycle of an information system is a difficult statement to verify, yet it is still an important issue that needs to be communicated. Therefore, it would be appropriate to use the "should" term in the policy statement. For example, "The organization should apply information system engineering principles in the specification, design, development, implementation, and modification of the information system."

- *Avoid the term "must."* The term "must" is generally intended to have the same definition as "shall" but contractually the term "shall" is generally accepted. In fact, the term "shall" has been held up in court, whereas the term "must" has not. One of the meanings of the term "must" is synonymous with "ought" and "should." Yes, the term "must" sounds stronger and more natural than the term "shall" but when writing policy statements, use the terms "shall," "will," and "should."

- *Policy statement references.* Many individual information security policy statements derive from standards, regulations, and other reference documents. It may be useful to provide a specific reference in each policy statement indicating the source of the policy statement or the intent to address a specific standard, regulation, or other source documents. It is also possible that a single policy statement may address multiple standards, regulations, or other source documents, in which case multiple references could be provided at the end of an information security policy statement. For example, the policy statement below indicates the source documents:

Disable Inactive Accounts. The department shall ensure the information system automatically disables inactive accounts after 90 days. For information systems containing cardholder data (CHD) the time period must be no more than 90 days. [NIST 800-53 AC-2(3)] [IRS Pub 1075] [PCI DSS 8.5.5].

4.2.1 Back Matter

Since many of the information security policy statements are derived from reference standards, regulations, and other source documents, a reference section should be added to the end of the policy document. The reference section allows those attempting to implement the policy statements to look up the source documents for clarity or supplemental guidance. The reference section also is a good record of the version and date of the source documents necessary to determine when the policy documents will need to be updated.

4.2.2 Policy Requirement Exceptions

There are times in which an organization (or a department within an organization) may realize that an information security policy requirement may not be reasonable or even possible to implement. In these cases, an information security policy requirement exception should be developed. The benefit of creating a policy exception is that the information security requirement is directly addressed and a documented rationale is provided explaining why the exception is requested or taken.

An information security policy exception is a gap between the information security requirements and the adopted information security policy. In most cases, information security policy will reflect information security requirements, but occasionally an organization may find it appropriate to document an exception to a requirement. Exceptions are generally noted with a modification to the requirement, with compensating controls, or with a risk-based rationale. Each of these information security policy exception types are explained below:

- *Exception with requirement modification.* This type of policy exception acknowledges the security requirement but provides a modification to the strength, frequency, or application of the requirement. For example, the policy statement below is modified to perform a review of selected audit events every 6 months instead of every year.

Audit reviews and updates. The department shall review and update the selected audited events annually, every 6 months, or as required.

- *Exception with compensating controls.* This type of policy exception acknowledges the security requirement, states that the requirement cannot (or will not) be met by the system, system component, or the department, and provides compensating controls to address residual risks of not implementing this control. For example, the policy statement below states that the identification and authentication requirement cannot be met by a system component and offers a list of compensating controls to offset the residual risk.

Identification and authentication of organizational users. The department shall ensure that the organization's information system uniquely identifies and authenticates organizational users (or processes acting on behalf of organizational users).

Exception: Thin-client workstations require a logon to provide access to applications. Group identifiers are used for thin clients.

Compensating controls

- Thin-client desktop has no access to sensitive data.
- Data may not be stored on thin-client desktops.
- Each application requires a unique user identifier and authentication credential to login.

- *Exception with risk-based rationale.* This type of policy exception acknowledges the security requirement, states that the requirement cannot (or will not) be met by the system, system component, or the department, and provides a risk-based rationale to address residual risks of not implementing this control. For example, the policy statement below states that the authentication feedback requirement cannot be met by a web-based application in the system and offers a rationale of why the risk is considered low for this component.

Authenticator feedback. The department shall ensure the state information system obscures feedback of authentication information during the authentication process to protect the information from possible exploitation/use by unauthorized individuals.

Exception: Web-based application has an option to "show password" while providing authentication information. Users are instructed to guard their screen and to only use this option when providing authentication information after a failed attempt. The risk of exposure is considered low based on limited use of the web application to a protected environment and user training provided for protection from shoulder surfing.

SIDEBAR: SELECTING COMPENSATING CONTROLS USING THE "9-CELL"

The selection of compensating controls can seem somewhat arbitrary or more of an art than science in that there are no set rules for the selection of these controls. In an effort to assist information security professionals with selecting these controls, the "9-Cell" approach is introduced here.

Step 1: Creating the "9-Cell"

A common approach to categorizing information security controls is to group them according to function. These functions are prevention, detection, and correction. The prevention grouping is for those controls that are designed to prevent an adverse security incident. The detection grouping is for those controls that are designed to detect when an adverse event has taken place. The correction grouping is for those controls that are designed to correct an adverse condition once it has taken place.

Another common approach to categorizing information security controls is to group them according to their type. These types are administrative, technical, and physical. Administrative controls are those controls that are policies, procedures, or activities. (Activities include controls such as penetration testing or security risk assessments.) Technical controls are controls based within the system such as passwords, encryption, and access controls. Physical controls are controls based on a physical device or personnel such as a fence or security guard.

To create a "9-Cell," simply create a 3-by-3 table with the columns labeled by the security control functions (preventative, detective, and corrective) and the rows labeled by the security control type (administrative, technical, and physical).

Step 2: Fill Out the "9-Cell"

To fill out the "9-Cell," consider each cell and the intersection of the security control function and grouping (e.g., preventative–administrative) and then consider any current or future controls that may compensate for the lack of the target control. For example, a requirement for the preventative–administrative cell would be a security control that is a policy, procedure, or activity that is designed to prevent an adverse event (e.g., acceptable use policy [AUP] and employee screening).

Step 3: Use the Completed 9-Cell to Brainstorm Compensating Controls

A completed 9-Cell contains multiple security controls that should be considered when building a set of compensating controls for a security requirement that cannot be met. As mentioned above, there is no exact science to select compensating controls but people tend to get stuck trying to replace a required control with a like control (e.g., replace a preventative-physical control such as a lock with another preventative-physical control such as solid-core door). As an example, consider a requirement for the encryption of sensitive data at reset for any device that leaves a protected area (e.g., a tablet with client files that goes home with a worker). As part of this example, assume that there is no built-in or available software to perform this encryption. If there is an overwhelming business need to accommodate the business practice of taking home such a device, then a set of compensating controls should be developed and deployed to reduce the risk. The original require- ment of encryption for data at rest is a "technical–preventative" control in the 9-Cell. The first impression is to select a compensating control from the same cell (e.g., custom software solution to encrypt the data at rest) but in reviewing the completed 9-Cell below, we see that a variety of solution sets of compensating controls could come out of this brainstorming exercise. The general rule of brainstorming is not to consider the feasibility of the solutions as you are generating ideas (e.g., self-destruct solution) but to continue to generate ideas to increase your ability to generate new ideas and create a larger-potential solution set (Table 4.2).

4.3 Specific Information Security Policies

Each organization has a unique culture, mission, threat environment, and a set of customer and industry regulations. Each organization has unique needs for information security policies. Therefore, informa- tion security policy development is not a one-size-fits-all approach

Table 4.2   9-Cell Example

9-CELL (TABLET DATA AT REST)	PREVENTATIVE	DETECTIVE	CORRECTIVE
Administrative	• Tablet acceptable use agreement	• Report lost/stolen tablet procedure	• Lost/stolen tablet recovery procedure
Technical	• Custom encryption software • Tablet authentication	• Tablet logon and access audit logs	• Remote wipe • Remote locator
Physical	• Tablet lock	• Tablet alarm on failed authentication	• Self-destruct on 24 h of no login

Note: A brainstorming exercise called "the 9-Cell" is implemented by creating a 3 × 3 table of security control functions and types and filling in each cell with a security control that meets the "type" and "function" pair. This exercise is useful in generating ideas for compensating security controls.

(or at least should not be). A complete set of example information security policies is described in Section 4.4. Example policies are contained in Appendix A. However, the reader is encouraged to create a unique set of information security policies that meets the specific needs of the target organization. This section provides some additional guidance on how these information policies are generally constructed.

4.3.1 Organizational-Level Policies

The foundational information security policies are referred to as organizational security policies. These policies establish the basic definition of sensitive information and how to handle it (e.g., data classification policy) and the roles and responsibilities of the information security function. Each of these policies are briefly outlined below:

- *Data classification and handling policy.* The data classification policy is a foundational policy because it defines what is meant by sensitive data and the associated responsibilities and minimum security controls for each classification category. The data classification policy can take on many forms but the basic structure should address the following topics:
  - *Data classification levels*: Define each data classification level (e.g., internal use only, proprietary, confidential, and restricted confidential) and include examples of data that would be included in the classification level.

- *Roles and responsibilities*: List the roles and responsibilities in the area of data classification. Roles may include the information security officer (responsible for developing policies and procedures for the security of classified data), the data owner (responsible for properly classifying data), and data custodian (responsible for implementing appropriate controls).
- *Data rules*: Data classifications must also have an accompanying set of rules that govern how they are treated. A data classification policy has an effect on the security and control of sensitive information only when it associates rules with each of the data classifications. Below is a list of data rules that may be applied to various data classification levels:
  - *Marking*: Sensitive data shall be labeled with the appropriate sensitivity level and any handling instructions necessary.
  - *Handling*: The data classification policy should dictate any limitations or requirements on hand carrying, receipt of delivery, data guardianship, out-of-sight procedures, and restricted conversations and movements.
  - *Transmission*: The data classification policy should dictate any limitations or requirements on transmission-encrypted transmissions and encryption algorithms and strength.
  - *Processing*: The data classification policy should dictate any limitations or requirements on approved processing devices.
  - *Storage*: The data classification policy should dictate any limitations or requirements on physical and logical requirements for storage.
  - *Disposition*: The data classification policy should dictate any limitations or requirements on information preservation, sanitization, disposal, and destruction.
- *Information security program policy.* The information security program policy is a foundational policy because it defines the

roles and responsibilities of the information security staff and the controls in place to establish, manage, and maintain an information security program. The information security program policy can take on many forms but the basic structure should address the following topics:

- *Roles and responsibilities*: The information security program policy should define the major roles and responsibilities for establishing, monitoring, and managing the information security program. This should include the CISO (if applicable), the information security manager (for each division), the incident response team, and other key roles in the security team.
- *Information security policies*: The information security program policy should identify the information security PSPs that are to be established and maintained.
- *Information system security plan*: The information security program policy should identify the organization's plan to define minimum controls for each information system, document compliance with minimum controls, and authorize changes and operation of the system.
- *Information security risk management*: The information security program policy should define controls to conduct, document, and review information security risk assessments for organizational information systems.
- *Security testing and monitoring*: The information security program policy should define controls for conducting, documenting, and reviewing security testing and monitoring activities.

4.3.2 Security Program-Level Policies

Once the basic information security program is established, a more detailed set of information security policies is required to detail the minimum controls in the information security program activities. These policies generally cover program topics such as incident response, security monitoring, contingency planning, and personnel security controls. Each of these policies are briefly outlined below:

- *Incident response.* The incident response policy can take on many forms but the basic structure should address the following topics:
  - *Incident response training*: The incident response policy should define the required training in terms of roles, topics, and frequency.
  - *Incident response testing*: The incident response policy should define the required testing of the incident response plan and capability in terms of testing types, involvement, and frequency.
  - *Incident handling*: The incident response policy should define the incident-handling capability required of the incident response team in terms of process, availability, roles, and activities.
  - *Incident monitoring*: The incident response policy should define the required monitoring in terms of roles, capability, and automation.
  - *Incident response plan*: The incident response policy should define the required documentation of the incident response roles, processes, metrics, reportable incidents, and team structure.
- *Contingency planning.* The contingency-planning policy can take on many forms but the basic structure should address the following topics:
  - *Contingency plan*: The contingency-planning policy should define the required elements of the contingency plan (e.g., recovery objectives, contact information, and critical assets).
  - *Training*: The contingency-planning policy should define the required training in terms of roles, topics, and frequency.
  - *Testing*: The contingency-planning policy should define the required testing of the incident response plan and capability in terms of testing types, involvement, and frequency.
  - *Alternative storage, processing, and telecommunications*: The contingency-planning policy should define the requirements for storage, processing, and telecommunications

to be used in the event of a disaster. These requirements should address contracts and agreements, environmental controls, access controls, and audit controls.

- *Backup*: The contingency-planning policy should define backup requirements for critical information systems.
- *Recovery and reconstitution*: The contingency-planning policy should define the requirements for recovery and reconstitution in terms of types of service and recovery objectives.

- *Personnel security controls.* The personnel security controls policy can take on many forms but the basic structure should address the following topics:

  - *Sensitive positions*: The personnel security controls policy should define sensitive positions within the organization and any additional personnel controls required for these positions.
  - *Employee screening*: The personnel security controls policy should define requirements for preemployment screening (e.g., background check, reference check, and credit check), frequency of rescreening, and actions to be taken based on the results of screening.
  - *Termination procedures*: The personnel security controls policy should define the process for ensuring that an employee departure maintains the security and privacy of organizational information systems and sensitive data (e.g., escort, account termination, service termination, and exit interviews).
  - *Sanctions*: The personnel security controls policy should define sanctions policy and process in place to ensure compliance with security and privacy policies.

4.3.3 User Security Policies

The basic information security policy directed at the user is the AUP. This policy dictates to the user the expectations and limits of using organizational computing resources. When composing an AUP, there are two important elements: the content and the organization of the content.

- *AUP content.* When creating a policy, it is best to ensure that the policy statements address all the associated requirements from the source documents (e.g., state and federal laws, industry standards, customer requirements, and business requirements). In the case of the AUP, there are relatively few source documents that address the contents. Many regulations merely state that you should have one and that it should inform the user of an acceptable use of technology. Regulations that do dictate AUP content are generally limited to the following:
  - *NIST 800-53*: Contains requirements for ensuring access agreements are created and signed, the use of unauthorized software, and unauthorized use of software
  - *Payment Card Industry's Data Security Standard (PCI DSS)*: Contains requirements for ensuring access agreements are created and signed
  - *Health Insurance Portability and Accountability Act (HIPAA) security rule*: Contains requirements for sanctions levied on noncompliant users
  - *State laws*: May contain requirements that prohibit tampering with computers, introducing malware, disrupting information systems, circumventing security controls, unauthorized access to or release of sensitive information, and unauthorized use of inappropriate material

  This leaves a lot of room for creating the needed content on advising the users on the acceptable use of technology. The balance of the AUP policy statements should provide the user with enough detail and direction that their responsibilities and limitations are well understood. The contents of the balance of the policy statements may be highly dependent on the target organization and the technology utilized. The AUP is typically one of the most highly customized documents for an organization in order to fit the corporate environment, mission, and culture.

- *AUP content organization.* It is important that the AUP be well organized to aid users in understanding the controls and expectations. Although there are many ways to organize the AUP, the following organization works very well and is recommended:

- *Expected behaviors*: This section covers behaviors that are expected of the user. For example, practicing safe computing, protecting sensitive information, and reporting suspicious behavior.
- *Prohibited behaviors*: This section covers behaviors that the user is prohibited from performing. For example, unauthorized and inappropriate use, tampering or circumvention of controls or information systems, and unauthorized messaging or use of sensitive information.
- *Notifications and acknowledgments*: This section notifies the user of the organization's ownership of system components and data, system monitoring, no expectations of privacy, and requires user acknowledgment of the agreement.
- *Riders (if necessary)*: Additional sections can be added for unique environments or user situations that require additional controls. For example, a home office agreement (additional physical and system controls expected at home).

4.3.4 System and Control Policies

The most detailed policies of the information security policy set are the system and control-level policies. These policies are also typically the most frequently updated policies because they are most closely related to changing technology. System and control-level policies are typically divided into topics such as network security, identification and authentication, access control, and system security audit. Some of the more common of these policies are briefly outlined below:

- *Network security*. The network security policy can take on many forms but the basic structure should address the following topics:
  - *Architectural controls*: The network security policy should define secure architectural controls such as boundary protection, implementation of a demilitarized zone (DMZ), and firewall configurations.
  - *Server controls*: The network security policy should define secure architectural controls such as minimum secure functions and secure configuration.

- *Service controls*: The network security policy should define secure architectural controls such as denial-of-service protection, cryptographic services, secure transmission, and protection of information at rest.
- *Identification and authentication.* The identification and authentication policy can take on many forms but the basic structure should address the topics of unique identification, authentication types and multifactor authentication, device identification, identifier management, and authenticator management.
- *Access control.* The access control policy can take on many forms but the basic structure should address the topics of access enforcement, access control operational procedures, least privilege, system use notification, session lock, and access restrictions (e.g., remote access, wireless access, and mobile device access).
- *System security audit.* The system security audit policy can take on many forms but the basic structure should address the topics of required audit events, audit event contents, audit record storage, audit record review, audit report generation, time stamp granularity, and protection of audit records.

4.4 Policy Document Examples

In general, information security policies should be developed for a specific organization based on its own mission, set of environmental threats, regulation environment, and company culture. Much of the text in this book discusses how to incorporate these aspects into the development or revision of a custom or tailored set of information security policies for a given organization. However, in an effort to provide a concrete example and demonstrate many of the elements discussed in this book, a set of example policies are provided in Appendix A.

It may be useful to the reader to understand the background of these example policies. These example policies are based on the policies created for the State of Arizona Department of Administration. The Arizona Department of Administration is responsible for providing information security policies for all the departments within the state.* The set of security policies provided here are the result of the security and privacy project for the Arizona Department of Administration. The framework chosen for the project was the National Institute of Standards and Technology's Special Publication 800-53 (Security and Privacy Controls for Federal Information Systems and Organizations).† Using the Federal Information Security Management Act (FISMA) (e.g., NIST 800-53 controls) as the framework for the policy set, several information security regulations and standards were also selected for inclusion in the initial policy set. These regulations and standards included the PCI DSS, the Security Rule of the HIPAA, and Tax Information Security Guidelines for Federal, State, and Local Agencies (Publication 1075).

Within each of these policies are several references or indicators that make the policy statements more useful and easy to apply.

Protected system requirement indicator (P). Each system in the state is determined to be a "standard" system or a "protected" system. Simply put, if the system stores, processes, or transmits sensitive information, then it is a protected system. All other information systems are standard. Requirements within the policy set that apply only to protected information systems are indicated with a "(P)" at the beginning of the requirement.

Source reference. Each of the policy requirements contains a source reference at the end of the requirement to indicate the source of the requirement. Many requirements have multiple sources as the security requirement is contained in multiple regulations and standards.

The example policy set contains 17 policies based on the FISMA framework. The policies are grouped into security management policies, security technical policies, security operational policies, and privacy policies, as illustrated in Table 4.3. For the purpose of clarity and brevity, the front matter and back matter, except for the policy purpose and scope, have been omitted from these examples.

---

* In the state of Arizona, not all state organizations are called departments. They are called budget units, which refers to departments, bureaus, and commissions.
† The original security and privacy policy project selected NIST 800-53 Rev 3. Three months into the project, NIST released Rev 4 and the project was revised to baseline the policy set on the new revision.

Table 4.3   Example Information Security Policy Set

POLICY#	DOCUMENT NAME	POLICY#	DOCUMENT NAME
SECURITY MANAGEMENT POLICIES		SECURITY OPERATIONAL POLICIES	
P8110	Data classification	P8210	Security awareness training
P8120	Information security program	P8220	System security maintenance
P8130	System security acquisition	P8230	Contingency planning
SECURITY TECHNICAL POLICIES		P8240	Incident response planning
P8310	Account management	P8250	Media protection
P8320	Access control	P8260	Physical security protection
P8330	System security audit	P8270	Personnel security protection
P8340	Identification and authentication	P8280	Acceptable use
P8350	System and communication protections	PRIVACY POLICIES	
		P8410	System privacy

Note: The information security policy example set consists of 17 information security and privacy policies based on the NIST 800-53 framework. These policies are grouped into security management policies, security technical policies, security operational policies, and security privacy policies.

EXERCISES

1. Using your own organization's information security policies (or a set given to you by your instructor), identify 10 uses of the terms *shall, will, should,* or *must.*
    a. Do you believe this is the appropriate and intended use of these terms?
    b. In what cases may the use of the term lead to confusion?
    c. If applicable, how would you rewrite each of these statements using the correct term?

2. Using your own organization or a fictitious company, create a roles and responsibilities matrix to differentiate the responsibility of the CIO, CISO, information security manager, and security administrator with respect to the following security controls:
    a. Development, review, revision, maintenance, and dissemination of information security policies.
    b. Performance of vulnerability scanning, creation and review of the scan report, and approval of a "clean" scan.
    c. Performance, oversight, and approval of an annual security risk assessment.
    d. Information security incident investigation.

3. Section 4.2.2 describes the information security policy exception process.
    a. What are the three exception types described?
    b. Give at least two reasons why it is important to document information security policy exceptions.
    c. Who should grant these exceptions?

4. This chapter introduces the concept of the "9-Cell" as a means to brainstorm compensating controls. Consider the following example information systems that require a compensating control-based exception and complete a 9-Cell to brainstorm potential compensating controls. Then write a compensating controls-based exception to the policy statement and exception pairs below:
    a. *Policy statement.* The department shall ensure the information system enforces password-based authentication with

a minimum strength of eight characters and one number or special character.

Exception: Specialized equipment has no capability of passwords beyond a four-digit PIN, contrary to the password policy statement above.

b. *Policy statement.* Scan for vulnerabilities in the organization information system and hosted applications quarterly from internal and external interfaces.

Exception: Production system is deemed critical and delicate in that the risk of vulnerability scans causing an error or disruption has been deemed too risky.

5

INFORMATION SECURITY PROCEDURES AND STANDARDS

The bulk of this book addresses information security policies—frameworks, statements, review, and projects. For the most part, all of the advice and guidance applied to information security policies (e.g., frameworks, terms, and audience) can also be applied to procedures and standards as well. This chapter addresses the specific elements of information security procedures and standards that are unique.

5.1 Less Formal Language and Structure

The formal language of information security policies (e.g., use of the term *shall*) may be dropped from these more detailed documents. Information security procedures and standards are not the formal documents of policy that need to stick with legal terms and standard templates but a more instructional and detailed document that provides guidance, variable settings, examples, and step-by-step instructions. For this reason, these documents are typically written in a less formal language and structure.

5.2 Various Purposes of the Standard and Guideline

Information security standards* and guidelines are a refinement of security requirements in the information security policies that address selected methods, techniques, and devices. Information security standards are developed to provide greater explanation or specificity for information security policy-level statements.

---

* Information security guidelines differ from information security standards only in that standards are mandatory and guidelines are not. For this reason, discussion on information security standards and guidelines development are treated nearly equal.

An information security standard or guideline may serve one or more purposes. These documents are the next level of detail from the information security policy. They may provide any one (or more) of the following purposes:

- *Specify control settings.* Information security standards (or guidelines) may provide more detailed specifications for information security control settings. Information security controls may require refinement and adjustment at a quicker pace than information security policies can be revised, approved, and adopted. Including the detailed specifications of information security controls to a standard or guideline allows quicker adoption of refinements to these controls.

  Examples of control settings appropriate for information security standards and guidelines include password strength and reuse settings, encryption strength settings, and audit event settings. Below is an example of a standard covering audit control setting and the topics of system audit capability, system audited events, unsuccessful logon attempts, and session lock.

Audit events. The department shall ensure that state information systems are capable of auditing the minimum set of events that may be required to support the department's auditing policy and those events listed under the "System Audit Capabilities" column in the table below. In addition, the department shall also ensure that the department information system is configured to audit the minimum set of events listed under the "System Audited Events" column in the table below [NIST 800-53 AU-2].

SYSTEM AUDIT CAPABILITIES	SYSTEM AUDITED EVENTS
Password changes	Password changes
Successful and failed logons [PCI DSS 10.2.5]	Successful and failed logons [PCI DSS 10.2.5] [IRS Pub 1075]
Successful system component access [PCI DSS 10.1]	Successful system component access [PCI DSS 10.1]
Failed system component access	Failed system component accesses

(Continued)

SYSTEM AUDIT CAPABILITIES	SYSTEM AUDITED EVENTS
Administrative privilege usage	Administrative privilege usage including changes to administrative account, administrative group account, escalation of user account to administrative account, and adding or deleting users from the administrator group accounts [IRS Pub 1075]
All actions taken by individuals with root or administrative privilege [PCI DSS 10.2.2]	All actions taken by individuals with root or administrative privilege [PCI DSS 10.2.2] [IRS Pub 1075]
Third-party credential usage	Third-party credential usage
Successful and failed access to system objects (e.g., files)	
Initialization or disabling of audit logs [PCI DSS 10.2.6] [IRS Pub 1075]	Initialization or disabling of audit logs [PCI DSS 10.2.6] [IRS Pub 1075]
Access to audit trails [PCI DSS 10.2.3]	Access to audit trails [PCI DSS 10.2.3] [IRS Pub 1075]
	Failed or successful access to system objects with confidential data [PCI DSS 10.2.1, 10.2.4]
Creation or deletion of system-level objects [PCI DSS 10.2.7]	Creation or deletion of system-level objects [PCI DSS 10.2.7]
	All changes to access control (e.g., rights and permissions) [IRS Pub 1075]
	Creation, modification, and deletion of objects including files, directories, user accounts, group accounts, and account privileges [IRS Pub 1075]
	Start up and shutdown functions [IRS Pub 1075]
	Command line changes, batch file changes, and system queries [IRS Pub 1075]

Unsuccessful logon attempts. The information system enforces the following parameters for unsuccessful logon attempts:

PARAMETER	VALUE
Limit of consecutive invalid logon attempts	6
Response to over limit invalid attempts	Automatically lock account/node
Lock-out period	30 min or release by administrator

(*P*) *Session lock.* The information system prevents further access to the system by enforcing the following parameters for session locks:

PARAMETER	VALUE
Initiate lock session after defined duration of inactivity or on user request	15 min
Retain session lock for defined duration or until user reestablishes access	30 min
Result of user not reestablishing session	Session dropped

- *Provide expanded guidance.* Some information security policy statements provide a requirement without details of how that requirement may be met. This is intentional as technology rapidly changes. It is typically useful to leave the system owners and custodians details of how to meet the requirement rather than attempting to spell out every detail in a security policy statement. However, this sometimes leaves the security practitioner with the difficult task of interpreting the meaning of the requirement. Information security standards can provide additional guidance in these situations.

  For example, consider the requirement, "The department shall ensure the information system protects against or limits the effects of denial of service (DoS) attacks." It may be unclear as to how the department may protect against or limit the effects of a DOS attack. Techniques and controls used today may not be relevant in the future. As DoS attacks continue to evolve, so must the department's response to them. A potential information security standard statement associated with this policy could address this requirement with some expanded guidance such as

> In order to limit the effects of DoS attacks, the department should address the following types of DoS and distributed denial of service (DDoS) attacks with known mitigation techniques. The list of DoS and DDoS attacks with known mitigation techniques includes the Internet Control Message Protocol (ICMP) Flood, Smurf Attack, SYN Flood, User Datagram Protocol (UDP) Flood, Teardrop Attack, domain name system (DNS) Amplification Attack, and Encrypted secure sockets layer (SSL) DDoS Attacks. In addition to implementing mitigation techniques for known DoS and DDoS attacks, the department should implement anomaly detection, if available on their equipment, to identify and mitigate new attacks. Anomaly detection requires the establishment of a baseline of network use to determine anomalies and potential attacks.

- *Provide example approaches.* Some information security policy statements provide a requirement without requiring a specific approach (e.g., penetration testing is required but no mention as to tools, techniques, or approaches). This is intentional as there may be many reasonable ways to implement the requirement and those may change over time. Organizations do not generally want to limit themselves to a specific technique, approach, or tool. However, in the absence of any guidance, departments may be stuck attempting to determine their own approach to meeting the policy requirement. In these cases, information security standards can introduce and detail a reasonable and accepted approach to meeting the requirement.

For example, an information security policy may have the following policy statements regarding information security risk assessments:

Security risk assessment. The department shall: [NIST 800-53 RA-3] [HIPAA 164.308 (a)(1)(ii)(A)]

1. Conduct an assessment of security risk, including the likelihood and magnitude of harm, from the unauthorized access, use, disclosure, modification, or destruction of the state information system and the information it processes, stores, or transmits
2. Document risk assessment results in a risk assessment report
3. Review risk assessment results annually [PCI DSS 12.1.3]
4. Disseminate risk assessment results to the department chief information officer (CIO), information security officer (ISO), information systems owner, and other department-defined personnel or roles
5. Perform the risk assessment annually, or whenever there are significant changes to the information system or environment of operations (including the identification of new threats and vulnerabilities), or other conditions that may impact the security state of the system [PCI DSS 12.1.2]

There are a great many approaches to performing an information security risk assessment. At the same time, there are a lot of approaches that fall short of being useful to the department in terms of completeness and depth. The organization (or the department) may consider the creation of an information security risk assessment standard to document minimum expectations of this service without limiting the variety of reasonable approaches such as

Security risk assessment guidance. The following guidance is provided for the performance of information security risk assessments. This guidance is presented within the context of the phases of an information security risk assessment process. Namely, the preparation, the performance, and the communication of the results for an information security risk assessment.

1. Information security risk assessment preparation. Preparation for an information security risk assessment helps to ensure that the department derives the most value from this exercise and establishes the context of the risk management process. Departments shall consider the following steps in preparing for an information security risk assessment:

   a. Identify purpose. The obvious purpose for an information security risk assessment is to provide system owners with information regarding the risk to sensitive data and critical information systems so that they may make appropriate decisions regarding how to address those risks. However, information security risk assessments are also required periodically based on applicable regulations, provide oversight to the security operations of the system, or could be the direct (and required) action from a recent audit or inspection. It is important that the department clearly understands and identifies the purpose of the information security risk assessment and conveys that to the team performing and overseeing the assessment in order to ensure project success.

   b. Define assessment boundaries. An information security risk assessment shall be limited to defined physical and logical boundaries. A physical boundary identifies the physical limit of the assessment such as network components (e.g., workstations, servers, routers, and switches), security components (e.g., intrusion detection system [IDS] and firewalls), network media (e.g., cabling), peripherals, buildings, and rooms. A logical boundary identifies the logical limit of the assessment such as the functions of the system, services provided, applications, and network segments.

c. Define level of rigor. An information security risk assessment shall have a defined level of rigor specifying the depth of analysis to be performed. The level of rigor may be specified by hours (or other resources metrics) to be expended or by listing the methods of data gathering.

d. Document scope limitations and constraints. An information security risk assessment is generally expected to cover all relevant administrative, technical, and physical controls. When the scope is limited or constraints are placed on the task of assessing the risk to the state information system, the budget unit needs to ensure that these constraints are reasonable. If a budget unit chooses to limit the scope of the risk assessment (e.g., physical security controls are out of scope), then there should be some rationale provided on why such a limitation is reasonable (e.g., physical security controls are reviewed under another assessment program).

e. Document risk model. There are a variety of reasonable security risk models that may be used in the performance of an information security risk assessment (e.g., NIST 800-30). The budget unit (or the contractor for the budget unit) may use any reasonable security risk model provided the model accounts for the following aspects of a baseline information security risk assessment:

   i. Document risk elements. The information security risk model shall identify and document the elements to be reviewed, assessed, and analyzed in order to determine the risk to the state information system. These elements typically include threats, assets, vulnerabilities, likelihood, and impact.

   ii. Document risk calculation. The information security risk model shall identify the process by which risk is determined. This is typically in the form of a risk calculation, estimate based on parameters, or a risk determination table based on the risk elements listed above.

Information security risk assessment performance. The effective performance of an information security risk assessment is critical to the accuracy and usefulness of the assessment. Departments shall consider the following steps in the performance of an information security risk assessment:

1. Objectivity. Consistent with requirement 6.5.1.1 of P8120 (information security program policy), an information security risk assessment shall be performed by impartial assessors or assessment teams. Impartiality requires that the assessment team have no conflict of interest between the development, selection, and/or operation of the security controls under assessment.

2. Adequate data gathering. An information security risk assessment shall have adequate data gathered on the controls within the physical and logical boundaries of the assessment. Adequacy of the data gathering is largely subjective but the departments shall be hesitant to rely on information security risk assessments that have too few data points to draw an accurate conclusion or assessments that rely on interviews of surveys alone from those in charge of the assessed controls. To the extent possible, the department should ensure that effective data gathering approaches from reviewing documents, interviewing

personnel, observing behavior, inspecting controls, and testing controls are utilized.

3. Defendable analysis. An information security risk assessment shall include a documented and defendable analysis of the data gathered to support findings. Information security risk assessments typically provide such analysis in the form of tables or charts. Each finding/recommendation shall be traceable to sufficient evidence of the vulnerability that is being addressed.

Information security risk assessment documentation. The effective and accurate communication of results from an information security risk assessment is critical to the usefulness of the assessment. Departments shall consider the following steps in the documentation of an information security risk assessment:

1. Communication with key staff. The results of an information security risk assessment provide pertinent information and guidance to system owners, information security officers, and CIOs within the budget unit. The results of the assessment shall be shared with budget unit director, CIO, information security officer, and system owners at a minimum. The state chief information security officer may also be included in the dissemination of the assessment results.

2. Communication with custodians and others. The results of the information security risk assessment include recommendations for improvements (e.g., patch information systems, develop procedures, and additional controls) that will need to be conveyed to those in charge of implementing these changes. When relevant, all available evidence of the associated vulnerabilities and details of the recommended solutions shall be made available to the system custodians, staff members, or contractors tasked with confirming the vulnerability and/or implementing the recommended solution. Keep in mind that the principle of least privilege shall be applied here and there

may be some details deemed irrelevant and sensitive and therefore not conveyed to others.

3. Clear recommendations. An information security risk assessment shall provide a report with clear recommendations that identify the control gap or risk and the recommended solution or solution set to address the control gap or risk. Departments may want to require that the information security risk assessment recommendations provide information on the cost of the recommendation as well.

5.3 Information Security Procedures

Information security procedures are instructions for the accomplishment of a process. The reason such instructions are documented is to ensure all elements of the procedure are completed and the procedure is executed in a uniform manner.

The creation of information security procedures is rather tedious but straightforward. There are few restrictions or set formats for procedures but there are a few simple rule or pieces of advice that may assist in their development:

- *Define process initiation and termination points.* Every process has a beginning and an end. These are referred to as initiation and termination points.

    An initiation point is defined by the information required to begin the process. There may be several initiation points; each should be defined. For example, the account creation process could have an initiation point of hiring a new employee, transferring an employee, or promoting an employee. Each of these initiation points should be defined in terms of the information required to initiate the process (e.g., employee name, employee identification number, job classification, location, and supervisor).

    A termination point is defined by the result of the process that marks its completion. There may be several termination points; each should be defined. For example, the account creation process could have the termination point of informing the employee of their new (or changed) account or denying the requested account access.

- *Document process steps.* Write down the steps involved in the process from beginning to end. This includes all initiation points, all termination points, and all the steps involved between. Flow charts work well for mapping this out and should be included in the process documentation.

- *Screenshots for computer-based process steps.* For all process steps that involve a computer program, include screenshots to improve the clarity and ease-of-use of the process document.

- *Document roles and responsibilities.* For each process step, document the party responsible for the completion of the step. "Swim lane" diagrams may be useful in some process documentation that involves multiple roles such as processes with approval or oversight activities.

- *Attach forms.* Many processes may involve a form to capture information more easily (e.g., account request and security incident report). A copy of the latest form should be included in the process documentation.

EXERCISES

What reasons are there to write mandatory elements of an information security policy in an information security standard instead?

1. Review the following information security standards and create a list of required procedures:
    a. Payment Card Industry Data Security Standard
    b. NIST Special Publication 800-53 (moderate level)
    c. ISO 27001 Clauses and Appendix A
    d. Control objectives for information and related technology
2. Review the security risk assessment guidance in section above.
    a. Was the last security risk assessment performed for your organization consistent with the guidance?
    b. In what way would you either modify the guidance to meet your current practices or modify your practices to meet the guidance?
3. Create a flow diagram for a process that does not currently exist within your organizations (pick one):
    a. Account creation and termination process
    b. Breach notification process
    c. Security incident reporting process
    d. Media disposal procedures
    e. Sanctions process

6

INFORMATION SECURITY
POLICY PROJECTS

Embarking on a project to revise or rearchitect an information security policy set for an organization is a large and complex enough project to warrant project planning. Determining the steps required to complete the project, setting a budget, and obtaining expertise and oversight are all important steps toward ensuring a successful completion of an information security policy project. This chapter outlines the basic elements of an information security policy project.

6.1 Scoping the Project

As with any project, an important early element of the project plan is to scope the project effort and extent. An information security policy project has the scoping aspects as listed in Table 6.1.

Of course, information security policy projects may vary widely in terms of effort. On the small end of the scale would be a small organization that is able to accept a ready-made set of information security policy templates with very little customization. Such a small project may only take a week or two and cost very little. However, the lack of customization and tailoring of the policies may result in an information security program that is not well suited for the organization's culture, industry, or threat environment.

On the higher end of the scale is a very large information security revision or rearchitect project for a large organization with many departments with different security needs. Such a project will likely have most or all of these scoping complexities. A project attempting to use a ready-made policy set to address an organization's needs would not likely meet the organization's goals for implementing security policies. Such a project could take several months or a year to complete.

Table 6.1   Information Security Policy Project Scoping Elements

POLICY PROJECT SCOPING ELEMENT	COMMENTS
Number of current policies	Current information security policies are the existing rules governing the protection of the system. These policies may be outdated but they are the current set of rules and will need to be reviewed as part of the policy revision or rearchitecting project.
Current policy framework	If the existing policy set does not have a clear and evident framework, the review and revision of these policies can be difficult. You will likely find many instances of conflicting policy statements, overlap, and gaps. This greatly increases review and approval time frames as the existing policy set and concerns about correctly translating it to a new policy set become complex.
Planned policy framework	If the planned policy framework has already been determined, the work of putting together policy statements into policies is relatively straightforward. If the policy framework is to be determined as part of the policy development project, then consider the time required to discuss the various choices of frameworks and the pros and cons of each.
Oversight and approval involvement	An approval stage for revising information security policies is necessary as these are statements of management intent. If there is a complex set of approvals or a very involved approval process, then the policy project will need to ensure there is considerable time devoted to the explanation, review, revision, and approval process.

Note: Not all information security projects are made alike. Depending on various complexities, some projects may be more involved and require a greater amount of time.

6.2 Information Security Policy Project Roles

There are several important roles in the information security policy project. These roles include the following:

- *Project sponsor.* As information security policies are the statement of management intent on the protection of information systems and data, it is required to obtain top management support and sponsorship of the project. The involvement of the role of top management (the project sponsor) is flexible. Smaller organizations will likely obtain an active role from the project sponsor while larger organizations may only touch base with the project sponsor during budgeting, major milestones, and the review and approval process.

- *Project lead.* The project lead is the expert in the development of information security policies. This person should have an in-depth knowledge of the information security regulations and requirements that affect the organization, experience with the selected information security framework chosen for the project, and experience in creating policy, standards, and procedure documents. The project lead will likely be the most influential person on the project as he will likely be the one with the most experience in the individual tasks required. As such, it is important that the project lead be skilled at identifying potential obstacles, outlining the choices to the other team members, and driving such decisions to a conclusion to keep the project on track and clear of common obstacles.

- *Subject matter expert (SME).* Information security policies will cover a wide range of information security topics. The project lead will likely not be an expert in all topic areas and will need some assistance to ensure proper interpretation of requirements and potential impact on the organization and the organization's information systems. In addition to providing subject matter expertise, involving the SME will help to reinforce organizational and departmental buy-in to the policies being developed.

- *Stakeholders.* Information security policies dictate how users are required to behave and how security controls are implemented within organizational information systems. These documents will affect a great many people and organizational processes. Among those most affected are the stakeholders such as department heads, system administrators, the department managers, and information security managers for each department. An information security project should seek to involve stakeholders in the project as much as possible by providing regular project status updates, involvement in the review process, and opportunities for training.

- *Approver.* Each information security policy may have one or more approvers. This could be a committee, the board, or senior management. It is important to understand the approval process prior to finalizing the information security project process as approvals may involve several steps and iterations over a period of time.

- *Technical editor.* Information security policies should follow the organizational template for formal documents. As these documents increase in size, so does the complexity of keeping within the confines of a prescribed document template. Involving a technical editor on the information security policy project team will smooth the development effort and save many hours of the project lead's time.

6.3 Information Security Policy Project Phases

As an example of an information security project that involved many of these complexities, consider the policy development project illustrated in Figure 6.1. A basic breakdown of this project includes the following nine phases:

- *Determine applicable laws, regulations, and standards.* The project began with a review of all known applicable laws and regulations. These included federal information security laws and regulations (e.g., Health Insurance Portability and Accountability Act Security and Privacy Rules, Federal Information Security Management Act, and National Institute of Standards and Technology [NIST] Special Publication 800-53), Arizona state laws and Arizona Revised Statues, and industry standards (e.g., Payment Card Industry Data Security Standard [PCI DSS]). Between federal, state, and industry laws, there were 63 applicable laws, regulations, and standards. Each of these documents was catalogued.
- *Identify best practice sources.* In addition to these laws, the project required the identification of sources for best practices (e.g., NIST Special Publications 800-series, Center for Information Security hardening guidelines, and internal organization practices). Each of these best practice sources was catalogued as well.
- *Review current policies, standards, and procedures (PSPs).* A formal review of the identified laws, regulations, and standards was then conducted to identify actionable content (e.g., policy statements, requirements, and guidance).

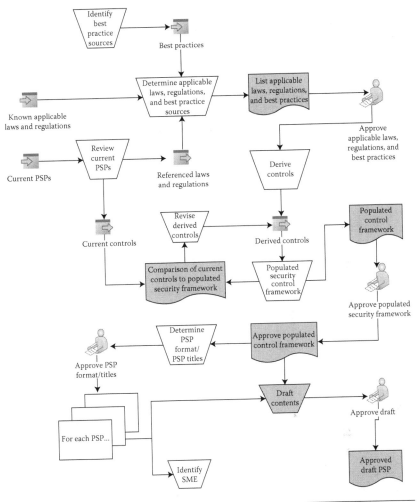

Figure 6.1 PSP development process—example. The example information security policy process involves identifying best practices and applicable laws, reviewing current policies, deriving security controls, populating the security control framework, and determining format and policy titles.

- *Derive controls.* The actionable content identified in each of the sources was then transformed (if necessary) into policy statements or security controls. This was done by naming each policy statement by the security control enforced (e.g., "password-based authentication") ensuring a straightforward language and consistent set of terms (e.g., shall).

- *Populate security control framework.* For this project, the FISMA framework was selected as the control framework. This framework was slightly modified from the FISMA framework identified in Figure 3.1 (see the difference between Figure 3.1 and Table 4.3). The revised framework provided a structure to organize the identified controls into control groups and eventually into individual information security policies (groupings of related control groups).

- *Revise derived controls.* The derived controls were then reviewed against the identified controls in the current information security PSPs. Based on this review, some controls were revised to accommodate a stronger control already in place.

- *Determine format and titles.* With the revised controls in place and sorted into the approved framework, controls were then grouped according to subject (e.g., network controls and user account controls) and audience (e.g., policies for all staff vs. policies limited to administrators). This sorting resulted in plans to develop 17 information security and privacy policies.

- *Identify SME.* For each policy, an SME was identified to provide expert review of the policies being developed. In addition to valuable reviews from someone who works with the controls directly affected by the draft policy, this is also an important part of the buy-in process. By involving the SME in the draft review and revision process, the policy (or procedure) becomes an extension of his or her own understanding of how the controls should be implemented.

- *Draft contents.* Once the policy titles, topics, and controls were created and approved, the contents of each document were drafted. These drafts are based on the approved information security policy framework and the approved security controls so the drafting of the policies concentrates on the combination, structuring, and wording of the policy statements.

6.4 Information Security Policy Revision Project

The balance of this chapter on information security policy projects assumes that information security policies are being rearchitected or created from scratch. In fact, most information security policy projects do involve rearchitecting the policy framework or starting from scratch so a complete project plan discussion is generally applicable. Even when initially seeking to simply revise an existing information security policy set, many projects end up rearchitecting the policy set because it is easier. There are several reasons why an information security policy project may be easier to rearchitect than to revise:

- *Old policy set.* Information security policy sets are typically designed to be revised on an annual basis. Those sets that fail to have routine maintenance are typically so far behind changes in technology, the organizational needs, and regulations that a simple revision is no longer the easy route. Generally, a set of information security policies that have not been revised for 3 or more years should be rewritten from scratch.
- *Lack of framework.* No matter how often an information security policy set is maintained and expanded, if it was built on an as-needed basis or otherwise built without regard to a clear structure and framework, then attempted revisions will soon become too complex. When attempting to expand an information security policy set that is created without a clear framework, it is not clear where additional policy statements belong. Lacking a clear place for the proposed new statements, organizations typically will simply create another policy title to house a small set of policy statements. This results in the "yet another policy" syndrome where users become so weary of the myriad of information security policies and keeping track of what is required that they simply give up on attempting to understand the rules of the organization.
- *Too many policies already.* Generally, organizations with 50 or more information security policies have been suffering from this syndrome for a while. It would be best to rearchitect the whole mess and provide a clear and consistent information security policy set.

However, occasionally, an information security policy project may only seek to revise or even add to an existing well-organized information security policy set. In this case, the information security project is one of revision and not rearchitecting, so the process is much simpler to discuss. There are four general reasons to revise an existing information security policy. Each of these is discussed below:

- *Audit findings.* When revising the information security policy set to address specific audit findings, the findings themselves are the driver of the project. If the audit findings indicate that the information security policies are nonexistent, out of date, or do not provide the details necessary to address information security requirements, then this is not a revision project but a rearchitect (or creation) project. However, if the audit findings are specific, simply track each finding to a missing, ambiguous, or incorrect policy statement and revise.

- *Policy currency review.* For information security policies that are being reviewed (within a few years) of the last policy review, this type of project involves SMEs to identify current issues, new threats, and additional controls that may need to be required by the policy set. A well-organized information security policy set will allow the project to focus on specific information security policies instead of the entire set. For example, if an organization feels the need for a currency review on its information security policy set due to the increased demand and use of consumer electronics in the workplace and at home utilizing organizational data, then a policy review may be limited to the Acceptable Use Policy, Media Protection Policy, and the System and Communication Protection Policy.

- *Policy consistency review.* As the set of information security policies grows and expands to include overlapping areas of concern, there is a threat of inconsistency within the policy set. This can happen when more than one information security policy addresses a specific security control. For example, the Acceptable Use Policy, the Email Policy, and the Security Awareness Training all provide the user with requirements or guidance on selecting a strong password. If each of these policies (and training) provides specifics on password strength (e.g., number of characters, selection of upper and lower case, and inclusion of a special character), then there is a danger that each may require (or suggest) something different. Such an inconsistency in a policy set leads to users dismissing policies and a degraded security posture.

A policy consistency review is best performed using a technique known as an *expected elements review*. In an expected elements review, a list of security controls (e.g., expected elements of the security policies) is used as a place holder to map the policy statement of each policy to a specific security control. This approach was originally presented in *The Security Risk Assessment Handbook* (2006).

- *Policy requirements review.* In a project that involves reviewing existing information security policies for compliance with a set of requirements (e.g., industry regulations or standards, customer requirements, and organizational requirements), the set of requirements is first reviewed to identify the requirements. Each requirement is then mapped to an existing policy statement in the information security policy set or the requirement is mapped to a target policy for inclusion. At the conclusion of the mapping, each existing information security policy will have an associated list of candidate requirements for inclusion. Working on the policies one after the other, the candidate requirements are then written into the existing policies. Again, if the existing information security policy set is well organized and based on an information security policy framework, the identification of the appropriate policy for each candidate requirement will be obvious. If it is difficult to perform this mapping, then a policy rearchitecting may be in order.

6.5 Information Security Policy Project Application

Once the information security policies are drafted, the policies must go through an approval process, organizational departments will require training on the policies, and additional policy application consulting will be required for some organizational departments. Figure 6.2 provides an example of the application process for the newly developed or revised PSPs. There are three major phases of the policy application process with three tasks in each phase.

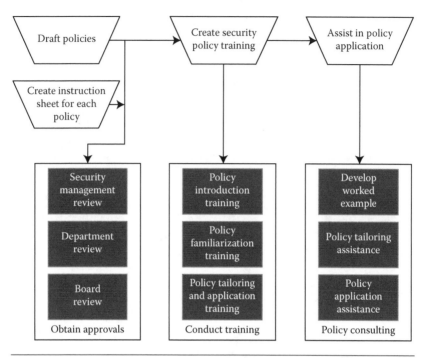

Figure 6.2 PSP application process—example. The example information security policy application process involves policy approval, policy training, and policy application consulting.

Phase 1: Policy approval. Once the PSPs are developed, the next phase is to seek formal approval. In addition to the draft policies, Figure 6.2 shows the step of creating a policy instruction sheet for each policy to aid in the review process. Figure 6.3 shows an example of a policy instruction sheet (or summary) that provides a single-page summary of the policy purpose, importance, audience, and high-level policy statements.

In smaller organizations, approval may be only a single step, but in larger organizations, approval must be sought through several steps, namely, security management review, department review, and board review.

- *Security management review.* This approval phase requires that the senior-most information security representative for the organization agrees with and approves the information security policy set, policy statements, and approach for policy governance. If the security policy set was developed within this department or team, then this task may have already been

Information Security Program

IT SECURITY POLICY 8120

Purpose:
Establish an information security program and determine the responsibilities within the agency.

Why it's important:
A comprehensive plan that defines the elements needed for a secure information security program. It ensures that information security risks are identified, addressed and documented.

Target audience:
All employees should understand the foundation of the requirements.

Overview:

- Develop, distribute, review and update an information system security plan that is consistent with the agency's enterprise architecture, defines authorized connected devices, provides an overview of the security requirements for the system, and outlines the security controls in place.

- Develop an information security architecture for the state information system that describes the philosophy, requirements, and approach to protecting the confidentiality, integrity and availability of information.

- Develop, document and disseminate all IT security policies to appropriate personnel. Maintain, review and update the policies as needed.

- Develop a strategy to manage risk to operations, assets, individuals and other organizations; perform impact assessments.

- Categorize state information systems according to the potential impact resulting from disclosure, destruction or unavailability of data.

- Develop a plan of action and milestones to document planned remedial actions to correct weaknesses or deficiencies during security controls assessment.

- Develop a continuous monitoring strategy and establish security metrics.

Conduct security risk assessments to identify the likelihood and magnitude of harm to the state information system.

Scan for vulnerabilities and implement remediation procedures.

Develop and maintain an inventory of information systems and classify all system components.

Facilitate ongoing security education and training for personnel.

Establish frequencies for monitoring and assessments.

Authorize internal system connections such as printers, laptops, and mobile devices.

For more information about this IT Security Policy, contact SecurityPolicies@azdoa.gov.

ADOA-ASET
Arizona Strategic Enterprise Technology

Figure 6.3 Information security policy summary—example. The policy summary provides a single-page summary of the policy purpose, importance, audience, and high-level policy statements.

completed with the completion of the draft policies, but if the policies have been created by an element of the team, another department, or an outside consultancy, then the senior-most security representative for the organization will have a formal approval process. The formal approval process may consist of a formal line-by-line presentation, discussion, and defense of each policy statement or it may simply be an offline review and revision of the drafted policies.

- *Department review.* This approval phase requires that the information security department of each organizational department receives a chance to provide input, clarification, or request modifications of the drafted policies. It is best to include these departmental representatives throughout the policy development process so that there are very few surprises. However, a formal and final review of these policies is typically necessary for organizations to take into account unique needs of each department and to help to ensure buy-in to the process.

- *Board review.* This is the final approval for policies but may not be necessary for standards and procedures. Policies are the statement of intent from senior management involving the secure use of organizational resources and protection of sensitive information. Therefore, senior management (e.g., the board or board delegate) must formally approve policy-level documents for the organization. Such approvals rarely include a line-by-line review but instead the board members typically rely on their own experts, subcommittees, and delegates to perform such a review and advisory role.

Phase 2: Policy training and consulting. Once the PSPs are approved by the security management, departments, and the board, training is required to provide appropriate guidance and understanding of the policies. Security policy training involves three steps: policy introduction training, policy familiarization training, and policy tailoring and application training.

- *Policy introduction training.* Information security policy introduction training is generally limited to the objectives of policy development project, the basics of the security policy framework chosen, and an outline of the policies and policy contents. Such a training session is generally limited to 1–2 h.

- *Policy familiarization training.* Security policy familiarization training explores each of the policies in more depth. This includes a review of the roles and responsibilities for each policy and a step-by-step review of each of the policy statements. Audience members will generally want to request an interpretation of some of the policy statements on their own information systems and/or comment on the impact of the policy statements on their department or information systems. Leaving time for such comments would require that this training take 4–6 h.

- *Policy tailoring and application training.* In addition to an in-depth policy training, many departments will require one-on-one training to discuss their own department's approach to tailoring and applying the information security policies to their department and department information systems. This type of training should be tailored to the department's specific questions and concerns but a general set of slides covering the following elements should be prepared and used as a consistent set of guidance to all departments:
  - *Roles and responsibilities*: Identify departmental roles (and names) to assign the roles and responsibilities from each policy. Example roles include department head, information technology lead, information security lead, and user manager.
  - *Department information systems*: Identify department information systems, including system name, function, and boundaries. This should include a discussion of the trade-offs between defining many small information systems versus several (or one) large system, and determining system owners.
  - *Adopting versus tailoring policy statements*: Each policy statement may either be adopted (e.g., the department agrees with the policy statement) or the department can request a policy exception (see Section 4.2.2).
  - *Completing policy statements*: Many policy statements may have been written to allow the department to specify, define, or assign an aspect of the policy statement. For example, consider the following policy statement: "The department information system automatically removes or disables temporary and emergency accounts after a department-defined time." The phrase department-defined time is to be replaced with a time period defined

by the department. For each of these phrases in a policy statement, the department will need to complete the policy statement with its own input. In order to assist departments with these decisions, it may be useful to create a tailoring guide that is used with all departments to ensure consistent advice. See *Appendix B: Example Departmental Policy Tailoring Guide* for an example of an instruction to departments on how to tailor information security policy templates for use in their organization.

Phase 3: Policy application and consulting. Once the information security policy training is complete, individual departments may require additional assistance or consulting in the development or application of their information security policies. The following consulting tasks are recommended for assisting these departments with the tailoring and application of their information security policies:

- *Develop a worked example*: A worked example (e.g., a completed policy set for a specific department) can provide other departments with guidance on how to complete a policy set. It is always useful to find a department willing to be held up as an example in exchange for assisting them with the development of their own policy set. This set can then be used as a worked example.
- *Provide policy tailoring assistance*: If the advice given in the training is not detailed or clear enough, some departments may require assistance with tailoring a policy set for their own department and department information systems. Assistance may involve selection of compensating controls or the development of a risk-based exemption rationale.
- *Provide policy application assistance*: Once the policy set is tailored and accepted by the department, it will then be applied to the department and its information systems. This means the development of security controls such as policies, procedures, processes, access controls, encryption, etc. Additional assistance to organizational departments may be useful to the overall organization in this area.

EXERCISES

1. Consider your own organization's information security policy set (or a set given to you by your instructor). Estimate the amount of time it would take to perform the following tasks:
   a. Update the policy set to include the latest version of PCI DSS
   b. Update the policy set for an update of the underlying framework (e.g., NIST 800-53, ISO 27001)
   c. Perform the review and approval process
2. When rearchitecting an information security policy set (e.g., creating a new set), why is it important to review the current set of information security policies?
3. What steps in an information security policy development project help to ensure organizational buy-in?
4. When adopting a new (or revised) information security policy, many departments and/or information systems may be noncompliant with the new security policy statements because they were previously not required.
   a. Is this a good reason for a department to request a policy exception?
   b. What reaction would you expect from an auditor for new requirements for an organization that has recently adopted new information security policies (e.g., organization has recognized new requirements but not yet implemented them)?

Appendix A: Example Policies (FISMA Framework)

The following set of information security policy examples are based on information security and privacy policies the author created for the State of Arizona Department of Administration. There are several elements of these example policies that are important to understand:

- *Application indicators*: Each policy statement required for all systems unless there is an application indicator at the front of the policy statement. All application indicators are enclosed in parenthesis at the front of the policy statement. Examples of these indicators include (C)—applies to confidential data only; (P)—applies to "protected" systems only; and (P-PCI)—applies to "protected" systems with cardholder data (CHD).
- *Source reference*: Each of the policy requirements contains a source reference at the end of the requirement to indicate the source of the requirement. Many requirements have multiple sources as the security requirement is contained in multiple regulations and standards. The source reference indicates both the source or the requirement and a requirement reference within that source (e.g., PCI DSS 12.1.3).

The example policy set contains 17 policies based on the FISMA framework. The policies are grouped into security management policies, security technical policies, security operational policies, and privacy policies. For the purpose of clarity and brevity, the front matter and back matter, except for the policy purpose and scope, has been omitted from these examples.

A.1 Information Security Management Policy Examples

Based on the Arizona Policy and Standards project, three policies were created to address the management of the information security program. These policies are directed at the classification of data, the information security program, and the secure acquisition of information systems, components, and services.

A.1.1 Policy Example: 8110 Data Classification

Purpose: The purpose of this policy is to provide a framework for the protection of data that are created, stored, processed, or transmitted within department. The classification of data is the foundation for the specification of policies, procedures, and controls necessary for the protection of confidential data.

Scope: This policy shall apply to all data, both paper copies and soft copy. Policy statements preceded by "(C)" are required for all confidential data.

A.1.1.1 Policy Statements   Data classification: Data created, stored, processed, or transmitted on organization information systems shall be classified according to the impact to the state or citizens resulting from the disclosure, modification, breach, or destruction of the data.

Data classification categories: All organization data shall be classified as one of the following categories: [National Institute of Standards and Technology Special Publication (NIST SP) 800-53 RA-2].

> *Confidential data*: Data that shall be protected from unauthorized disclosure based on laws, regulations, and other legal agreements. Examples of confidential data include
> 1.   System security parameters and vulnerabilities
>   a.   System security vulnerabilities

    b. Generated security information

    c. Information regarding current deployment, configuration, or operation of security products or controls

2. Health information

    a. Protected health information [Health Insurance Portability and Accountability Act (HIPAA)—PL 104-191, Sections 261–264, 45 Code of Federal Regulations (CFR) Part 160 and 164]

    b. Medical records [A.R.S. 12-2291, A.R.S. § 12-2292, A.R.S 36-445.04, A.R.S. § 36-404, A.R.S. § 36-509, A.R.S. § 36-3805]

    c. Child immunization data [A.R.S. § 36-135]

    d. Chronic disease information [A.R.S. § 36-133]

    e. Communicable disease information [A.R.S. § 36-664, A.R.S. § 36-666]

    f. Developmental disabilities service records [A.R.S. § 36-568.01, A.R.S. § 36-568.02]

    g. Emergency medical service patient records [A.R.S. § 36-2220]

    h. Genetic testing records [A.R.S. § 12-2801, A.R.S. § 12-2802]

    i. Home health service records [A.R.S. § 36-160]

    j. Midwifery patient records [A.R.S. § 36-756.01]

    k. State trauma registry [A.R.S. § 36-2221]

    l. Tuberculosis control court hearing information [A.R.S. § 36-727]

    m. Vital records [A.R.S. § 36-342]

3. Financial account data (on individuals)

    a. CHD, including primary account number, cardholder name, expiration date, and service code [PCI DSS v2.0]

    b. Credit card, charge card, or debit card numbers; retirement account numbers; savings, checking, or securities entitlement account numbers [A.R.S. § 44-1373]

4. Criminal justice information

    a. Child protective services records [A.R.S. § 41-1959]

    b. Criminal history record information [A.R.S. § 41-619.54]

    c. Criminal justice information [A.R.S. § 41-1750]

5. Critical infrastructure/fuel facility reports [A.R.S. § 41-4273]
6. Eligible persons [A.R.S. § 39-123, A.R.S. § 39-124]
7. Risk assessment and state audit records
   a. Auditor general records [A.R.S. § 41-1279.05]
   b. Federal risk assessments of infrastructure [A.R.S. § 39-126]
8. Personal identifying information (except as determined to be public record) [A.R.S. § 41-4172]
   a. Educational records [Family Educational Rights and Privacy Act]
   b. Social security number [A.R.S. § 44-1373]
9. Taxpayer information—federal tax information (FTI) [A.R.S. § 42-2001] [Internal Revenue Service Publication 1075 (IRS Pub 1075)]
10. Licensing, certification, statistics, and investigation information (of a sensitive nature)
    a. Abortion reports [A.R.S. § 36-2161]
    b. Child death records [A.R.S. § 36-3503]
    c. Controlled substance records [A.R.S. § 36-2523]
    d. Emergency medical service investigation records [A.R.S. § 36-2220]
    e. Employment discrimination information [A.R.S. § 41-1482]
    f. Healthcare cost containment records [A.R.S. § 36-2917]
    g. Healthcare directives registry information [A.R.S. § 36-3295]
    h. Healthcare entity licensing information [A.R.S. § 36-2403, A.R.S. § 36-404]
    i. Medical marijuana records [A.R.S. § 36-2810]
    j. Medical practice review [A.R.S. § 36-445, A.R.S. § 36-445.01]
    k. Nursing home certification records [A.R.S. § 36-446.10]
    l. Prescription information [A.R.S. § 36-2604]
11. Other state-owned confidential data may include, but not be limited to
    a. Archaeological discoveries [A.R.S. § 39-125]
    b. Attorney general opinions [A.R.S. § 38-507]

    c. Tax examination guidelines [A.R.S. § 42-2001]

    d. Unclaimed property reports [A.R.S. § 44-315]

    e. Vehicle information [A.R.S. § 41-3452]

12. Other non-state-owned confidential data may include, but not limited to

    a. Attorney–client privileged information [A.R.S. § 41-361]

    b. Bank records [A.R.S. § 6-129]

    c. Trade secrets and proprietary information [Intellectual Property laws]

    d. Management and support information

13. Other records protected by law

Public data: In accordance with Arizona public record's law, data that may be released to the public and requires no additional levels of protection from unauthorized disclosure.

Identification: All data shall be identified as one of the following data classifications:

1. Confidential or
2. Public (data that is not identified is assumed to be public)

A.1.1.1.1 Handling

(C) *Need to know*: All confidential data shall only be given to those persons who have authorized access and a need to know the information in the performance of their duties [HIPAA 164.308 (a)(3)(ii)(A)—Addressable] [PCI DSS 7].

(C) *Hand carry*: All confidential data being hand-carried shall be kept with the individual and protected from unauthorized disclosure.

(C) *Accounting*: For bulk transfer of confidential data containing 500 or more records, the receipt and delivery of all confidential data shall be monitored and accounted for to ensure the data are not lost and potentially compromised.

(C) *Guardian*: When outside of controlled areas, all confidential data shall not be left unattended, even temporarily. All confidential data shall remain either in a controlled environment or in the employee's physical control at all times. Mail, courier, or other mail services are considered controlled areas.

(C) *Out-of-sight*: All confidential data shall be turned over or put out of sight when visitors not authorized to view data are present.

(C) *Conversations*: Confidential data shall not be discussed outside of controlled areas when visitors not authorized to hear confidential data are present.

(C) *Movement*: Unauthorized movement of confidential data from controlled areas shall be prohibited [HIPAA 164.310 (d)(1)].

A.1.1.1.2 Transmission

(C) *Encryption*: Any external transmission of confidential data shall be encrypted through either link or end-to-end encryption [HIPAA 164.308 (e)(2)(ii)—Addressable] [PCI DSS 4].

(C) *Encryption strength*: Encryption algorithm and key length shall be compliant with current state organization minimum encryption standards as stated in the System and Communications Protection Standard [S8350].

A.1.1.1.3 Processing

(C) *Approved processing*: Confidential data shall be processed on approved devices.

A.1.1.1.4 Media Protection

(C) *Confidential data protection*: All confidential data shall be protected and implemented at minimum controls as stated in the Media Protection Policy P8250 and Media Protection Standard S8250 [HIPAA 164.310 (d)(2)] [PCI DSS 3, 9].

A.1.2 Policy Example: 8120 Information Security Program

Purpose: The purpose of this policy is to establish the information security program and responsibilities within the department.

Scope: The policy shall apply to all organization information systems:

- (P)—Policy statements preceded by "(P)" are required for department information systems categorized as protected.
- (P-PCI)—Policy statements preceded by "(P-PCI)" are required for department information systems with PCI data (e.g., CHD).

- (P-PHI)—Policy statements preceded by "(P-PHI)" are required for department information systems with protected healthcare information.
- (P-FTI)—Policy statements preceded by "(P-FTI)" are required for department information systems with federal taxpayer information.

A.1.2.1 Policy Statements   System security planning: The department shall implement the following controls in the planning of system security:

System security plan: The department shall develop, distribute, review annually, and update an organization information system security plan. The plan shall [NIST 800-53 PL-2]
1. Be consistent with the department's enterprise architecture (EA)
2. Explicitly define the authorization boundary for the system, including authorized connected devices (e.g., smart phones, authorized virtual office computer equipment, and defined external interfaces)
3. Describe the operational context of the organization information system in terms of missions and business processes
4. Provide the security categorization of the information system
5. Describe the relationships with or connections to other information systems
6. Provide an overview of the security requirements for the system
7. Describe the security controls in place or planned for meeting those requirements, including rationale for the tailoring and supplementation decisions
8. Be reviewed and approved by the department chief information officer (CIO) prior to plan implementation
   (P) *Coordinate with other organizational entities:* The department shall plan and coordinate security-related activities affecting the organization information system with the department CIO, department ISO, and system owners of affected organization information systems

before conducting such activities in order to reduce the impact on other organizational entities [NIST 800-53 PL-2(3)] [IRS Pub 1075]

(P) *Information security architecture*: The department shall [NIST 800-53 PL-8] [IRS Pub 1075]
1. Develop an information security architecture for the organization information system that describes
   a. The overall philosophy, requirements, and approach to be taken with regard to protecting the confidentiality, integrity, and availability of organizational information
   b. How the information security architecture is integrated into and supports the EA
   c. Any information security dependencies on, and assumptions regarding, external services
2. Annually, review and update the information security architecture to reveal updates in the EA
3. Ensure that planned information security architecture changes are reflected in the security plan and organizational procurements/acquisitions

System security policies: The department shall develop, document, and disseminate, to appropriate personnel and roles, the following policies and procedures for each organization information system: [HIPAA 164.316 (a)]

1. Data classification policy and procedures (P8110)
2. Information security program policy and procedures (P8120) [NIST 800-53 CA-1] [NIST 800-53 PL-1] [NIST 800-53 PM-1] [NIST 800-53 RA-1]
3. System security acquisition policy and procedures (P8130) [NIST 800-53 SA-1]
4. Security awareness training policy and procedures (P8210) [NIST 800-53 AT-1]
5. System security maintenance policy and procedures (P8220) [NIST 800-53 CM-1] [NIST 800-53 MA-1] [NIST 800-53 SI-1]
6. Contingency planning policy and procedures (P8230) [NIST 800-53 CP-1]

7. Incident response planning policy and procedures (P8240) [NIST 800-53 IR-1]

8. Media protection policy and procedures (P8250) [NIST 800-53 MP-1]

9. Physical security protection policy and procedures (P8260) [NIST 800-53 PE-1]

10. Personnel security policy and procedures (P8270) [NIST 800-53 PS-1]

11. Acceptable use policy, including social media and networking restrictions (P8280) [NIST 800 53 AC-1] [NIST SP 800 53 PL-4(1)]

12. Account management policy and procedures (P8310)

13. Access controls policy and procedures (P8320) [NIST 800-53 AC-1] [HIPAA 164.310 (a)(2)(ii)]

14. System security audit policy and procedures (P8330) [NIST 800-53 AU-1]

15. Identification and authentication policy and procedures (P8340) [NIST 800-53 IA-1]

16. System and communication protections policy and procedures (P8350) [NIST 800-53 SC-1]

17. System privacy policy and procedures (P8410)

18. System privacy notice (S8410)

   Policy maintenance and distribution: The department shall [HIPAA 164.316 (b)(1), (b)(2)]

   1. Maintain the organizational security policies and procedures

   2. Retain these documents for 6 years from the date of its creation or the date it last was in effect, whichever is later. However, all state departments must comply with Arizona State Library, Archives and Public Records rules and implement whichever retention period is most rigorous, binding, or exacting

   3. Make documentation available to those persons responsible for implementing the procedures to which the documentation pertains

   4. Review documentation periodically, and update as needed, in response to environmental or operational changes affecting the security of the confidential information

Security risk management: To appropriately manage security risk to organization information systems, the following activities shall be performed for each organization information system: [HIPAA 164.308 (a)(1)(i), (a)(1)(ii)(B)]

Impact assessment: A potential impact assessment shall be performed for each organization information system to determine the system categorization. An impact assessment considers the data sensitivity and system mission criticality to determine the potential impact that would be caused by a loss of confidentiality, integrity, or availability of the organization information system and/or its data. Impact assessments result in the determination of impact based on the following definitions:

1. *Limited adverse impact*: The loss of confidentiality, integrity, or availability could be expected to have limited adverse effect on organizational operations, organizational assets, or individuals. For example, it may
   a. Cause a degradation in mission capability, to an extent and duration, that the organization is able to perform its primary function, but the effectiveness of the function is noticeably reduced
   b. Result in minor damage to organizational assets
   c. Result in a minor financial loss
   d. Result in minor harm to individuals
2. *Serious adverse impact*: The loss of confidentiality, integrity, or availability could be expected to have a serious adverse effect on organizational operations, organizational assets, or individuals. For example, it may
   a. Cause a significant degradation in mission capability, to an extent and duration, that the organization is able to perform its primary function, but the effectiveness of the function is significantly reduced
   b. Result in significant damage to organizational assets
   c. Result in a significant financial loss
   d. Result in significant harm to individuals that do not involve loss of life or serious life-threatening injuries

Note: Impact assessment on organization information systems storing, processing, or transmitting confidential data may result in a serious adverse impact.

System security categorization: The department shall categorize organization information systems, document the security categorization results (including supporting rationale) in the security plan for the organization information system, and ensure that the security categorization decision is reviewed by the department CSO and approved by the department CIO. All organization information systems are categorized according to the potential impact to the state or citizens resulting from the disclosure, modification, destruction, or nonavailability of system functions or data [NIST 800-53 RA-2].

System categorization levels: The following system categorization levels shall be applied to all organization information systems:

1. *Standard*: Loss of confidentiality, integrity, or availability could be expected to have a limited adverse impact on the department's operations, organizational assets, or individuals, including citizens

2. *Protected*: Loss of confidentiality, integrity, or availability could be expected to have serious, severe, or catastrophic adverse impact on organizational, assets, or individuals, including citizens

Security risk assessment: The department shall [NIST 800-53 RA-3] [HIPAA 164.308 (a)(1)(ii)(A)]

1. Conduct an assessment of security risk, including the likelihood and magnitude of harm, from the unauthorized access, use, disclosure, modification, or destruction of the organization information system and the information it processes, stores, or transmits

2. Document risk assessment results in a risk assessment report

3. Review risk assessment results annually [PCI DSS 12.1.3]

4. Disseminate risk assessment results to the department CIO, department ISO, organization information system owner, and other department-defined personnel or roles

5. Perform the risk assessment annually or whenever there are significant changes to the information system or environment of operations (including the identification of new threats and vulnerabilities), or other conditions that may impact the security state of the system [PCI DSS 12.1.2]

(P) *Third-party risk assessment:* The department shall conduct an assessment of risk, including the likelihood and magnitude of harm, from the unauthorized access, use, disclosure, modification, or destruction of third parties authorized by the department to process, store, or transmit confidential data [HIPAA 164.308 (a)(ii)(A)]

Vulnerability scanning: The department shall [NIST 800-53 RA-5] [PCI DSS 11.2]

1. Scan for vulnerabilities in the organization information system and hosted applications quarterly and when new vulnerabilities potentially affecting the system/applications are identified and reported from internal and external interfaces

2. Employ vulnerability scanning tools and techniques that facilitate interoperability among tools and automate parts of the vulnerability management process by using standards for
   a. Enumerating platforms, software flaws, and improper configurations
   b. Formatting checklists and test procedures
   c. Measuring vulnerability impact

3. Analyze vulnerability scan reports and results from security control assessments

4. Remediate legitimate vulnerabilities within 30 days in accordance with an organization assessment of risk

5. Share information obtained from the vulnerability scanning process and security control assessments with department-defined personnel or roles to help eliminate similar vulnerabilities in other organization information systems (i.e., systemic weaknesses or deficiencies)

6. (P) Establish a process to identify and assign risk ranking to newly discovered security vulnerabilities [PCI DSS 11.2]

(P) *Update tool capability:* The department shall employ vulnerability scanning tools that include the capability to readily update the organization information system vulnerabilities to be scanned [NIST 800-53 RA-5(1)] [IRS Pub 1075]

(P) *Update prior to new scans:* The department shall update the organization information system vulnerabilities scanned prior to new scans [NIST 800-53 RA-5(2)] [IRS Pub 1075]

(P) *Provide privileged access*: The organization information system implements privileged access authorization to department-defined components containing highly confidential data (e.g., databases) [NIST 800-53 RA-5(5)] [IRS Pub 1075]

(P) *Qualify scanning vendors*: The department shall employ an impartial and qualified scanning vendor to conduct quarterly external vulnerability scanning. The assessors or assessment team is free from any perceived or real conflict of interest with regard to the development, operation, or management of the department information systems under assessment and is qualified in the use and interpretation of vulnerability scanning software and techniques [PCI DSS 11.2.2]

Information security program management: The department shall implement the following controls in the management of the information security program:

Senior information security officer: The department shall appoint a senior information security officer with the mission and resources to coordinate, develop, implement, and maintain a department-wide information security program [NIST 800-53 PM-2] [EO 2008-10].

Information security resources: The department shall include the resources needed to implement the information security program and document all exceptions to this requirement. This includes employing a business case to record the resources required, and ensuring that information security resources are available for expenditure as planned.

Plan of action and milestones process: The department shall [NIST 800-53 PM-4]

1. Implement a process for ensuring that plans of action and milestones for the security program and associated organization information systems are
   a. Developed and maintained
   b. Reported in accordance with reporting requirements
   c. Documented with the remedial information security actions to adequately respond to risk to organizational operations, assets, individuals, other organizations, and the state
2. Review plans of action and milestones for consistency with the organizational risk management strategy and department-wide priorities for risk response actions

Information systems inventory: The department shall develop and maintain an inventory of its information systems, including a classification of all system components (e.g., standard or protected) [NIST 800-53 PM-5].

Information security measures of performance: The department shall develop, monitor, and report on the results of information security measures of performance [NIST 800-53 PM-6].

EA: The department shall develop the enterprise architecture with consideration for information security and resulting risk to organizational operations, organizational assets, individuals, other organizations, and the organization [NIST 800-53 PM-7].

Critical infrastructure plan: If applicable, the department shall address information security issues in the development, documentation, and updating of a critical infrastructure and key resources protection plan [NIST 800-53 PM-8].

Risk management strategy: The department shall

1. Develop a comprehensive strategy to manage risk to organizational operations and assets, individuals, other organizations, and the organization associated with the operation and use of organization information systems
2. Implement this strategy consistently across the organization [NIST 800-53 PM-9]

Security authorization process: The department shall [NIST 800-53 PM-10]

1. Manage the security state of organizational information systems and the environments in which those systems operate through security authorization processes
2. Designate individuals to fulfill specific roles and responsibilities within the organizational risk management process
3. Fully integrate the security authorization processes into a department-wide risk management program

Mission/Business process definition: The department shall [NIST 800-53 PM-11]

1. Define mission/business processes with consideration for information security and the resulting risk to organizational operations, organizational assets, individuals, other organizations, and the organization
2. Determine information protection needs arising from the defined mission/business processes and revises the process as necessary, until achievable protection needs are obtained

Insider threat program: The department shall implement an insider threat program that includes a cross-discipline insider threat incident handling team [NIST 800-53 PM-12].

Information security workforce: The department shall establish an information security workforce development and improvement program [NIST 800-53 PM-13].

Testing, training, and monitoring: The department shall [NIST 800-53 PM-14]

1. Implement a process for ensuring that organizational plans for conducting security testing, training, and monitoring activities associated with organizational information systems are developed and maintained; and continue to be executed in a timely manner.
2. Review testing, training, and monitoring plans for consistency with the organizational risk management strategy and department-wide priorities for risk response actions.

Contacts with security groups and associations: The department shall establish and institutionalize contact with selected

groups and associations within the security community to [NIST 800-53 PM-15]
1. Facilitate ongoing security education and training for department personnel
2. Maintain currency with recommended security practices, techniques, and technologies
3. Share current security-related information, including threats, vulnerabilities, and incidents

Security assessments and authorizations: The department shall implement the following controls in the assessment and authorization of organization information systems:

Security assessments: The department shall [NIST 800-53 CA-2] [HIPAA 164.308 (a)(8)]
1. Develop a security assessment plan that describes the scope of the assessment, including security controls under assessment, assessment procedures to be used to determine security control effectiveness, and assessment environment, assessment team, and assessment roles and responsibilities
2. Assess the security controls in the information system and its environment of operation periodically to determine the extent to which the controls are implemented correctly, operating as intended, and producing the desired outcome with respect to meeting established security requirements
3. Produce a security assessment report that documents the results of the assessment
4. Provide the results of the security control assessment to the department CIO, department CSO, and the state CSO
   (P) *Independent assessors*: The department shall employ impartial assessors or assessment teams to conduct security control assessments. The assessors or assessment team is free from any perceived or real conflict of interest with regard to the development, operation, or management of the department information systems under assessment [NIST 800-53 CA-2(1)] [IRS Pub 1075]

(P) *Third-party security assessment*: The department shall conduct a security assessment with third parties authorized by the department that process, store, or transmit confidential data [HIPAA 164.308 (a)(8)].

(P) *Wireless access point (AP) testing*: The department shall test for the presence of wireless access points and detect unauthorized wireless access points on a quarterly basis [PCI DSS 11.1].

System interconnections: The department shall [NIST 800-53 CA-3]

1. Authorize connections from the organization information system to other information systems through the use of interconnection security agreements

2. Document, for each interconnection, the interface characteristics, security requirements, and the nature of the information communicated

3. Review and update interconnections security agreements annually

   (P) *Restrictions on external system connections*: The department shall employ a "deny-all, permit-by-exception" policy for allowing protected organization information systems to connect to external information systems [NIST 800-53 CA-3(5)] [IRS Pub 1075]

   (P) *Third-party authorization*: The department shall permit a third party, authorized by the department to process, store, or transmit confidential data, to create, receive, maintain, or transmit confidential information on the department's behalf only if covered entity obtains satisfactory assurances that the third party will appropriately safeguard the information. The department documents the satisfactory assurance through a written contract or other arrangement with the third party [HIPAA 164.308 (b)(1) and (b)(2)]

Plan of action and milestones: The department shall [NIST 800-53 CA-5]

1. Develop a plan of action and milestones for the organization information system to document the organization's planned remedial actions to correct weaknesses or deficiencies noted during the assessment of the security controls and to reduce or eliminate known vulnerabilities in the system

2. Update existing plan of action and milestones annually based on the findings from security controls assessments, security impact analyses, and continuous monitoring activities

Security authorization: The department shall [NIST 800-53 CA-6]
1. Assign a senior-level executive or manager as the authorizing official for the information system
2. Ensure the authorizing official authorizes the organization information system for processing before commencing operations
3. Update the security authorization every 3 years

Continuous monitoring: The department shall develop a continuous monitoring strategy and implement a continuous monitoring program that includes [NIST 800-53 CA-7] [HIPAA 164.308 (a)(1)(ii)(D)]
1. Establishment of security metrics to be monitored
2. Establishment of frequencies for monitoring and frequencies for assessments supporting such monitoring
3. Ongoing security control assessments in accordance with the department continuous monitoring strategy
4. Ongoing security status monitoring of the department-defined metrics in accordance with the department continuous monitoring strategy
5. Correlation and analysis of security-related information generated by assessments and monitoring
6. Response actions to address results of the analysis of security-related information
7. Reporting the security status of the department and the information system to the state chief information security officer (CISO) quarterly

(P) *Penetration testing*: The department shall conduct penetration testing annually on protected organization information systems from internal and external interfaces. These penetration tests must include network-layer penetration tests and application-layer penetration tests [NIST 800-53 CA-8] [PCI DSS 11.3].

(P) *Independent penetration agent or team*: The department shall employ an impartial penetration agent or penetration team to perform penetration testing. The assessors or assessment team is free from any perceived or real conflict of interest with regard to the development, operation, or management of the department information systems under assessment [NIST 800-53 CA-8].

Internal system connections: The department shall authorize internal connections of other organization information systems or classes of components (e.g., digital printers, laptop computers, and mobile devices) to the organization information system and, for each internal connection, shall document the interface characteristics, security requirements, and the nature of the information communicated [NIST 800-53 CA-9] [IRS Pub 1075].

A.1.3 Policy Example: 8130 System Security Acquisition

Purpose: The purpose of this policy is to establish adequate controls for the acquisition and deployment of department information systems.

Scope: The policy shall apply to all organization information systems:

- (P)—Policy statements preceded by "(P)" are required for department information systems categorized as protected.

A.1.3.1 Policy Statements Allocation of resources: The department shall [NIST 800 53 SA-02]

1. Determine information security requirements for the organization information system or information system service in mission/business process planning
2. Determine, document, and allocate the resources required to protect the organization information system or information system service as part of its capital planning and investment control process

3. Establish a discrete line item for information security in organizational programming and budgeting documentation

Technology life cycle: The department shall [NIST 800 53 SA-03]

1. Manage the organization information system using a department-defined technology life cycle that incorporates information security considerations [PCI DSS 6.3]
2. Define and document information security roles and responsibilities throughout the technology life cycle
3. Identify individuals having information security roles and responsibilities
4. Integrate the organizational information security risk management process into technology life cycle activities

Software development process: The department shall require developers of organization information systems or system components to implement the following software development processes [PCI DSS 6.3]:

1. Remove nonproduction application accounts, user IDs, and passwords before applications become active or are released to customers
2. Review custom code prior to release to production or customers in order to identify any potential coding vulnerability

(P) *Change control procedures:* The department shall require developers of organization information systems, or system components to follow change control processes and procedures for all changes to system components. The process must ensure [PCI DSS 6.4]

1. Separate development/test and production environments
2. Separation of duties between development/test and product environments
3. Production data are not used for testing or development
4. Removal of test data and accounts before production systems become active

(P) *Secure coding guidelines*: The department shall require developers of organization information systems, or system components, to develop applications based on secure coding guidelines to prevent common coding vulnerabilities in software development processes, to include the following [PCI DSS 6.5]:

1. Injection flaws, particularly structured query language (SQL) injection (also consider operating system (OS) command injection, lightweight directory access protocol (LDAP) and XPath injection flaws, as well as other injection flaws)
2. Buffer overflow
3. Insecure cryptographic storage
4. Insecure communications
5. Improper error handling
6. All "high" vulnerabilities identified in the vulnerability identification process
7. For web applications and web application interfaces:
   a. Cross-site scripting (XSS)
   b. Improper access control (such as direct object references, failure to restrict uniform resource locator (URL) access, and directory traversal)
   c. Cross-site request forgery

Acquisition process. The department shall include the following requirements, descriptions, and criteria, explicitly or by reference, in the acquisition contract for the information system, system component, or information system service in accordance with applicable federal and state laws, executive orders, directives, policies, regulations, standards, guidelines, and organizational mission/business needs [NIST 800 53 SA-04]:

1. Security functional requirements
2. Security strength requirements
3. Security assurance requirements
4. Security-related documentation requirements
5. Requirements for protecting security-related documentation
6. Description of the information system development environment and environment in which the system is intended to operate
7. Acceptance criteria

(P) *Functional properties of security controls:* The department shall require the developer of the organization information system,

system component, or information system service to provide a description of the functional properties of the security controls to be employed [NIST 800 53 SA-04(1)] [IRS Pub 1075].

(P) *Design/implementation information for security controls*: The department shall require the developer of the organization information system, system component, or organization information system service to provide design and implementation information for the security controls to be employed that includes [NIST 800 53 SA-04(2)] [IRS Pub 1075].

1. Security-relevant external system interfaces
2. High-level design

(P) *Services in use:* The department shall require the developer of the organization information system component, or organization information system service, to identify early in the system development life cycle, the functions, ports, protocols, and services intended for organizational use [NIST 800 53 SA-04(9)] [IRS Pub 1075].

State information system documentation: The department shall [NIST 800 53 SA-05]

a. Obtain administrator documentation for the organization information system, system component, or organization information system service that describes
   1. Secure configuration, installation, and operation of the system, component, or service
   2. Effective use and maintenance of security functions/mechanisms
   3. Known vulnerabilities regarding configuration and use of administrative (i.e., privileged) functions
b. Obtain user documentation for the organization information system, system component, or organization information system service that describes
   1. User-accessible security functions/mechanisms and how to effectively use those security functions/mechanisms
   2. Methods for user interaction, which enables individuals to use the system, component, or service in a more secure manner

3. User responsibilities in maintaining the security of the system, component, or service

4. Protect documentation as required, in accordance with the risk management strategy

5. Ensure documentation is available to department-defined personnel or roles

(P) *Security engineering principles*: The department shall apply information system security engineering principles in the specification, design, development, implementation, and modification of the organization information system [NIST 800 53 SA-08] [IRS Pub 1075].

External information system services: The department shall [NIST 800 53 SA-09]

1. Require that providers of external organization information system services comply with organizational information security requirements and employ security controls in accordance with applicable federal and state laws, executive orders, directives, policies, regulations, standards, and guidance

2. Define and document government oversight and user roles and responsibilities with regard to external information system services

3. Employ service-level agreements (SLAs) to monitor security control compliance by external service providers on an ongoing basis [HIPAA 164.308(b)(1), 164.314(a)(2)(i)]

Identification of services: The department shall require providers of external organization information system services to identify the functions, ports, protocols, and other services required for the use of such services [NIST 800 53 SA-09(2)] [IRS Pub 1075]

(P) *Develop configuration management*: The department shall require the developer of the organization information system, system component, or organization information system service to [NIST 800 53 SA-10] [IRS Pub 1075]

1. Perform configuration management during system, component, or service (development, implementation, and operation)

2. Document, manage, and control the integrity of changes to configuration items under configuration management
3. Implement only department-approved changes to the organization information systems
4. Document approved changes to the system, component, or service and the potential security impacts of such changes
5. Track security flaws and flaw resolution within the system, component, or service

(P) *Develop security testing and evaluation*: The department shall require the developer of the organization information system, system component, or organization information system service to [NIST 800 53 SA-11] [IRS Pub 1075]

1. Create and implement a security assessment plan that provides for security testing and evaluation, at the depth of security-related functional properties, including
   a. Security-related externally visible interfaces
   b. High-level design
   c. At the rigor of demonstrating
2. Perform integration and regression testing for components and services and unit, integration, and system testing for systems
3. Produce evidence of the execution of the security assessment plan and the results of the security testing/evaluation
4. Implement a verifiable flaw remediation process
5. Correct flaws identified during security testing/evaluation
   (P) *Public web application protections*: The department shall require the provider of organization information system service for public-facing web applications to address new threats and vulnerabilities on an ongoing basis and to ensure that these applications are protected against known attacks by either of the following methods [PCI DSS 6.6]:
   1. Reviewing public-facing web applications using manual or automated application vulnerability security assessment tools or methods, at least annually and after any changes, or
   2. Installing a web application firewall in front of public-facing web applications

(P) *Threat and vulnerability analyses*: The department shall require the developer of the organization information system, system component, or organization information system service to perform threat and vulnerabilities analyses and subsequent testing/evaluation of the as-built system, component, or service [NIST 800 53 SA-11(2)] [IRS Pub 1075]

(P) *Independent verification of assessment plans/evidence*: The department shall require an independent agent to verify the correct implementation of the developer security assessment plan and the evidence produced during security testing/evaluation [NIST 800 53 SA-11(3)] [IRS Pub 1075]

(P) *Penetration testing/analysis*: The department shall require the developer of the organization information system, system component, or organization information system service to perform penetration testing to include black box testing by skilled security professionals simulating adversary actions and with automated code reviews [NIST 800 53 SA-11(5)] [IRS Pub 1075] [PCI DSS 6.3.2]

A.2 Information Security Operational Policy Examples

Based on the Arizona Policy and Standards project, eight policies were created to address the operations of the information security program. Operational policies cover the day-to-day operations of the information security program such as training, incident response, and physical and personnel controls.

A.2.1 Policy Example: 8210 Security Awareness Training and Education

Purpose: The purpose of this policy is to ensure all organization employees and contractors are appropriately trained and educated on how to fulfill their information security responsibilities.

Scope: This policy shall apply to all organization information systems:

- (P)—Policy statements preceded by "(P)" are required for organization information systems categorized as protected

- (P-FTI)—Policy statements preceded by "(P-FTI)" are required for organization information systems with federal taxpayer information

A.2.1.1 Policy Statements   Security awareness program development: The department ISO or assigned delegate shall define, document, and develop a security awareness training and education program for the department. The security training awareness and education program shall include the following elements:

(P) *Identify sensitive positions*: Identification of positions, systems, and applications with significant information security responsibilities and identification of specialized training required to ensure personnel assigned to these positions or having access to these systems and/or applications are appropriately trained [HIPAA 164.308(a)(5)(i)]
1. *Role-based security training*—Security training with appropriate content based on specific information security-related assigned roles and responsibilities [NIST 800 53 AT-3 supplemental guidance]

Workforce training: The department shall provide training to each member of the workforce.

(P-FTI) *FTI training*: Security training granted access to social security administration (SSA)-provided information shall include all of the topics listed in "specialized security training" below.

Security topics: Coverage of information security topics and techniques sufficient to ensure trained personnel comply with information security policies, standards, and procedures (PSPs).

(P) *Periodic security reminders:* Communication with employees and contractors providing updates to relevant information security topics or PSPs [HIPAA 164.308(a)(5)(ii)(A)].

Security awareness program operations: The department ISO or assigned delegate shall operate the security awareness training and education program for the department. The operations of the security training awareness and education program shall implement the following objectives:

Basic security awareness training: All employees and contractors shall complete security awareness training prior to being granted access to organization information systems, when required by information system changes [NIST 800-53 AT-2 b], and at least annually thereafter [PCI 12.6.1, NIST 800-53 AT-2 a, c].

(P) *Basic privacy training*: All employees and contractors shall complete privacy awareness training on the policies and procedures with respect to personally identifiable information (PII) prior to being granted access to such data and upon a material change in the policies and procedures [HIPAA 164.530(b)].

Specialized security awareness training: All employees and contractors shall receive relevant specialized training within 60 days of being granted access to organization information systems.

1. (P-FTI) The department shall establish and/or maintain an ongoing function that is responsible for providing security awareness training for employees granted access to SSA-provided information. Training shall include discussion of

   a. The sensitivity of SSA-provided information and address the Privacy Act and other federal and state laws governing its use and misuse

   b. Rules of behavior concerning use of and security in systems processing SSA-provided data

   c. Restrictions on viewing and/or copying SSA-provided information

   d. The employee's responsibility for proper use and protection of SSA-provided information, including its proper disposal

   e. Security incident reporting procedures

   f. The possible sanctions and penalties for misuse of SSA-provided information

   g. Basic understanding of procedures to protect the network from malware attacks

   h. Spoofing, phishing, and pharming scam prevention

2. (P-FTI) The department shall provide security awareness training annually or as needed and have in place administrative procedures for sanctioning employees up to and including termination of those who violate laws governing the use

and misuse of SSA-provided data through unauthorized or unlawful use or disclosure of SSA-provided information.

   a. Each user is required to sign an electronic version of the affirmation statement (terms and conditions for use) after reviewing the training. The agreement is captured and stored by the training coordinator.

   b. The user affirmation statement includes reference to state and federal law and sanctions that include dismissal and/or prosecution.

Security responsibilities: All employees and contractors shall be trained and educated in their information security responsibilities.

Acceptable use rules: All employees and contractors shall understand the acceptable use requirements of the organization information system, available technical assistance, and technical security products and techniques.

Training material: Information security awareness training and education material shall be developed, available for timely delivery, and generally available to all organization employees and contractors.

Training delivery: Security awareness training and educational material shall be delivered in an effective manner.

Security awareness program management and maintenance: The department ISO or assigned delegate shall manage and maintain the security awareness training and education program for the department. The security training awareness and education program management and maintenance activities shall include the following elements:

Tracking: Shall have effective tracking of security awareness training and education compliance for all employees and contractors with access to organization information systems, which includes periodic refresher training and education [NIST 800 53 AT-4].

   1. *Training records*—Training records shall be retained for 3 years [NIST 800 53 AT-4 supplemental guidance]. However, all state departments must comply with Arizona State Library, Archives and Public Records rules

and implement whichever retention period is most rigorous, binding, or exacting.

Acknowledgment: All employees or contractors who complete security awareness training and education programs shall acknowledge and accept that they have read and understood the organization information system requirements around information security policy and procedures [PCI 12.6.2].

Program updates: The security awareness training and education program shall be periodically reviewed and updated to reflect changes to information security threats, techniques, requirements, responsibilities, and changes to the rules of the system.

Security groups and associations: The department ISO or assigned delegate shall stay informed in the security community by establishing contact with selected groups and associations within the security community to facilitate training, and maintain currency with recommended practices and techniques [NIST 800 53 AT-5].

Feedback: The department ISO shall ensure an appropriate mechanism exists for feedback to the quality and content of the security awareness training and education program.

1. *Attendee review of security awareness training*: All employees or contractors who complete security awareness training and educational programs shall have an effective way to provide feedback. Contact information shall be made available to provide feedback at any time.

2. *Lessons learned*: Lessons learned from incident response and investigations shall drive improvements to the security awareness training and education program where relevant.

A.2.2 Policy Example: 8220 System Security Maintenance

Purpose: The purpose of this policy is to establish the baseline controls for management and maintenance of organization information system controls.

Scope: This policy shall apply to all organization information systems:

- (P)—Policy statements preceded by "(P)" are required for organization information systems categorized as protected.

A.2.2.1 Policy Statements

A.2.2.1.1 System Configuration Management

Configuration management plan: The department shall develop, document, and implement a configuration management plan for organization information systems that will

1. Address the roles, responsibilities, and configuration management processes and procedures

2. Establish a process for identifying configuration items throughout the software development life cycle and for managing the configuration of the configuration items

3. Define the configuration items for the organization information system and place the configuration items under configuration management

4. Protect the configuration management plan from unauthorized disclosure and modification [NIST 800 53 CM-9]

Baseline configuration: The department shall develop, document, and maintain a current baseline configuration of each organization information system [NIST 800 53 CM-2].

(P) *Baseline configuration reviews and updates*: The department shall review and update the baseline configurations for information systems, at least annually, upon significant changes to system functions or architecture, and as an integral part of system installations and upgrades [NIST 800-53 CM-2 (1)] [IRS Pub 1075].

(P) *Baseline configuration retention*: The department shall retain at least one previous version of baseline configurations to support rollback [NIST 800 53 CM-2 (3)] [IRS Pub 1075]. However, all state departments must comply with Arizona State Library, Archives and Public Records rules and implement whichever retention period is most rigorous, binding, or exacting.

(P) *Baseline configuration for high-risk areas*: The department shall establish separate baseline configurations for identified high-risk areas [NIST 800-53 CM-2 (7)] [IRS Pub 1075].

(P) *Change control board*: The department shall [NIST 800 53 CM-3] [IRS Pub 1075].

1. Determine the types of changes to the organization information system that are configuration controlled
2. Review proposed configuration-controlled changes to the organization information system and approves or disapproves such changes with explicit consideration for security impact analysis
3. Document configuration change decisions associated with the organization information system
4. Implement approved configuration-controlled changes to the information system
5. Retain activities associated with configuration-controlled changes to the organization information system in compliance with Arizona State Library, Archives and Public Records rules and implement whichever retention period is most rigorous, binding, or exacting
6. Coordinate and provide oversight for configuration control activities through an established configuration control board that convenes at least monthly to review the activities associated with configuration-controlled changes to organization information systems

Change approval: The department shall review and approve/disapprove proposed configuration-controlled changes to the organization information systems. Security impact analysis shall be included as an element of the decision [NIST 800 53 CM-4].

(P) *Test, validate, and document changes:* Approved changes shall only be implemented on an operational system after the change control board ensures that the change has been tested, validated, and documented [NIST 800 53 CM-4 (3)] [IRS Pub 1075].

(P) *Change restriction enforcement*: The department shall ensure that adequate physical and/or logical controls are in place to enforce restrictions associated with changes to organization information systems. The department shall permit only qualified and authorized individuals to access organization information systems for the purpose of initiating changes, including upgrades and modifications [NIST 800 53 CM-5] [IRS Pub 1075].

Configuration settings: The department shall [NIST 800 53 CM-6]

1. Establish and document configuration settings for information technology (IT) products employed within the organization information system using statewide, department-wide, or organization information specific security configuration checklists that reflect the most restrictive mode consistent with operational requirements

2. Implement the configuration settings

3. Identify documents, and approve any deviations from established configuration settings for all information system components for which security checklists have been developed and approved

4. Monitor and control changes to the configuration settings in accordance with organizational policies and procedures

Department information system component inventory: The department shall develop and document an inventory of organization information system components that accurately reflects the current organization information system, is consistent with the defined boundaries of the organization information system, is at the level of granularity deemed necessary for tracking and reporting hardware and software, and includes hardware inventory specifications (e.g., manufacturer, device type, model, serial number, and physical location), software license information, software version numbers, component owners, and for networked components: machine names and network addresses [NIST 800 53 CM-8].

Inventory reviews and updates: The department shall review and update the information system component inventory annually and as an integral part of component installations, removals, and information system updates [NIST 800 52 CM-8 (1)].

(P) *Inventory automated detection:* The department shall employ automated mechanisms to detect, quarterly, the presence of unauthorized hardware, software, and firmware components within the organization information system and take actions to disable network access, isolate the component, or notify the appropriate department personnel of the unauthorized component [NIST 800 53 CM-8 (3)] [IRS Pub 1075].

Software usage restrictions: The department shall use software and associated documentation in accordance with contract agreements and copyright laws; track the use of software and associated documentation protected by quantity licenses to control copying and distribution; and control and document the use of peer-to-peer file sharing technology to ensure that this capability is not used for the unauthorized distribution, display, performance, or reproduction of copyrighted work [NIST 800 53 CM-10].

Department information system maintenance: In addition to the change management requirements of Section 6.1, the following requirements apply to the maintenance of organization information systems:

Controlled maintenance: The department shall [NIST 800 53 MA-2]
1. Schedule, perform, document, and review records of maintenance and repairs on organization information system components in accordance with manufacturer or vendor specifications and department requirements.
2. Approve and monitor all maintenance activities whether performed onsite or remotely and whether the equipment is serviced onsite or removed to another location.
3. Explicitly approve the removal of the organization information system or system components from the department facilities for offsite maintenance or repair.
4. Ensure equipment removed from the department facilities is properly sanitized prior to removal (refer to Media Protection Policy P8250 for appropriate sanitization requirements and methods).
5. Check all potentially impacted security controls to verify that the controls are still functioning properly following maintenance or repair actions. These checks are documented in department maintenance records.

(P) *Maintenance tools:* The department shall approve, control, and monitor organization information system maintenance tools [NIST 800 53 MA-3] [IRS Pub 1075].

(P) *Tool inspection*: Maintenance tools and/or diagnostic and test programs carried into a department facility by maintenance personnel shall be inspected for improper or unauthorized modifications, including malicious code prior to the media being used in the organization information system [NIST 800 53 MA-3(1)(2)] [IRS Pub 1075].

Remote maintenance: The department shall [NIST 800 53 MA-4]

1. Approve and monitor remote maintenance and diagnostic activities
2. Allow the use of remote maintenance and ensure diagnostic tools are consistent with department policy and documented in the security plan for the organization information system
3. Employ two-factor authentication for the establishment of remote maintenance and diagnostic sessions
4. Maintain records for all remote maintenance and diagnostic activities in compliance with Arizona State Library, Archives and Public Records rules and implement whichever retention period is most rigorous, binding, or exacting
5. Terminate network sessions and connections upon the completion of remote maintenance and diagnostic activities

(P) *Remote maintenance policies and procedures*: The department shall document in the security plan for the organization information system the policies and procedures for the installation and use of remote maintenance and diagnostics are documented connections (see Information Security Program Policy P8120) [NIST 800 53 MA-4(2)] [IRS Pub 1075]

Maintenance personnel: The department shall [NIST 800 53 MA-5]

1. Establish a process for maintenance personnel authorization and maintain a list of authorized maintenance organizations or personnel
2. Ensure nonescorted personnel performing maintenance on organization information systems have required access authorizations
3. Designate organizational personnel with required access authorizations and technical competence to supervise the

maintenance activities of personnel who do not possess the required access authorizations

System and information integrity [HIPAA 164.132(c),(1)]

Flaw remediation: The department shall [NIST 800 53 SI-2]
1. Identify, report, and correct information system flaws
2. Test software and firmware updates related to flaw remediation are tested for effectiveness and potential side effects prior to installation
3. Install security-relevant software and firmware updates and patches within 30 days of release from the vendor
4. Incorporate flaw remediation into the organizational configuration management process

(P) *Automated flaw remediation system*: The department shall employ an automated mechanism monthly to determine the state of the information system components with regard to flaw remediation [NIST 800 53 SI-2(2)] [IRS Pub 1075].

Malicious code protection: The department shall [NIST 800 53 SI-3] [HIPAA 164.308(a)(5)(ii)(B)—Addressable] [PCI DSS 5.1]
1. Employ centrally managed malicious code protection mechanisms at organization information system entry and exit points and all systems commonly affected by malicious software particularly personal computers and servers to detect and eradicate malicious code [NIST 800 53 SI-3(2)]
2. Update malicious code protection mechanisms automatically whenever new releases are available in accordance with the department's configuration management policy and procedures [NIST 800 53 SI-3(1)]
3. Address the receipt of false positives during malicious code detection and eradication and resulting potential impact on the availability of the organization information system
4. Configure malicious code protection mechanisms to
   a. Perform periodic scan of the organization information system weekly and real-time scans of files from external sources at the endpoint, and network entry and exit points as the files are downloaded, opened, or executed

   b. Block and quarantine malicious code and/or send an alert to a system administrator in response to malicious code detection

   c. Generate audit logs [PCI DSS 5.3]

Information system monitoring: The department shall [NIST 800 53 SI-4a] [HIPAA 164.308(a)(1)(iii)(D)] [PCI DSS 11.4]

1. Monitor the organization information systems to detect attacks and indicators of potential attacks and unauthorized local, network, and remote connections

2. Identify unauthorized use of the organization information system through department-defined intrusion-monitoring tools

3. Deploy monitoring devices strategically within the organization information system, including at the perimeter and critical points inside the environment, to collect essential security-relevant data and to track specific types of transactions of interest to the department [PCI DSS 11.4]

4. Protect information obtained from intrusion-monitoring tools from unauthorized access, modification, and deletion

5. Heighten the level of monitoring activity within the intrusion-monitoring information systems whenever there is an indication of increased risk to organizational operations and assets, individuals, other organizations, or the organization based on confidential information

6. Receive alerts from malicious code protection mechanisms

7. Receive alerts from intrusion detection or prevention systems

8. Receive alerts from boundary protection mechanisms such as firewalls, gateways, and routers

9. Obtain legal opinion with regard to information system monitoring activities in accordance with applicable federal and state laws, executive orders, directives, policies, or regulations

   Updates: All intrusion detection systems and/or prevention engines, baselines, and signatures shall be kept up-to-date [PCI DSS 11.4].

(P) *Automated tools*: The department shall employ automated tools to support near real-time analysis of events [NIST 800-53 SI-4(2)] [IRS Pub 1075].

(P) *Inbound and outbound traffic*: The department shall monitor inbound and outbound communications traffic for unusual or unauthorized activities or conditions [NIST 800 53 SI-4(4)] [IRS Pub 1075].

(P) *System-generated alerts*: The department shall implement the information monitoring system to alert system administrators when the following indications of compromise or potential compromise occur [NIST 800 53 SI-4(5)] [IRS Pub 1075] [PCI DSS 11.4]:

Security alerts, advisories, and directives: The department shall implement a security alert, advisory, and directive program to [NIST 800 53 SI-5]

1. Receive information security alerts, advisories, and directives from and additional services as determined necessary by the department ISO on an ongoing basis

2. Generate internal security alerts, advisories, and directives as deemed necessary

3. Disseminate security alerts, advisories, and directives to appropriate employees and contractors, other organizations, business partners, supply chain partners, external service providers, and other supporting organizations as deemed necessary

4. Implement security directives in accordance with established time frames or notify the issuing organization of the degree of noncompliance

(P) *Integrity verification tools*: The department shall employ integrity verification tools to detect unauthorized changes to critical system files, configuration files, or content files [NIST 800 53 SI-7] [IRS Pub 1075] [HIPAA 164.312(c)(1)] [PCI DSS 11.5].

(P) *Integrity checks*: The department shall ensure organization information systems will perform integrity checks at least weekly and at start up, the identification of a new threat to which organization information systems are susceptible, and the installation of new hardware, software, or firmware [NIST 800-53 SI-7(1)] [IRS Pub 1075] [PCI DSS 11.5].

(P) *Incident response integration*: The department shall incorporate the detection of unauthorized changes to critical system files into the department incident response capability [NIST 800-53 SI-7(7)] [IRS Pub 1075].

Spam protection: The department shall employ spam protection mechanisms at organization information system entry and exit points to detect and take action on unsolicited messages and updates spam protection mechanisms automatically updated when new releases are available [NIST 800-53 SI-8, 8(2)] [IRS Pub 1075].

1. *Central management*: Spam protection mechanisms are centrally managed [NIST 800-53 SI-8(1)] [IRS Pub 1075].

(P) *Information input validation*: The department shall ensure organization information systems check the validity of information system inputs from untrusted sources such as user input [NIST 800-53 SI-10] [IRS Pub 1075].

Error handling: The department shall ensure the organization information system generates error messages that provide information necessary for corrective actions without revealing information that could be exploited by adversaries and reveals error messages only to system administrator roles [NIST 800-53 SI-11] [IRS Pub 1075].

Output handling and retention: The department shall handle and retain information within the organization information system and information output from the system in accordance with applicable federal and state laws, executive orders, directives, policies, regulations, standards, and operational requirements [NIST 800-53 SI-12] [Arizona Revised Statutes (ARS) 44-7041] [Arizona State Library Retention Schedules for IT Records].

A.2.3 Policy Example: 8230 Contingency Planning

Purpose: The purpose of this policy is to minimize the risk of system and service unavailability due to a variety of disruptions by providing effective and efficient solutions to enhance system availability.

Scope: This policy shall apply to all organization information systems:

- (P)—Policy statements preceded by "(P)" are required for organization information systems categorized as protected.

A.2.3.1 Policy Statements Develop contingency plan. The department shall develop a contingency plan that [NIST 800-53 CP-2] (HIPAA) 164.308(a)(7)(i), 164.308(a)(7)(ii)(b), 164.308(a)(7)(ii)(c), 164.310(a)(2)(i)]

1. Identifies essential mission and business functions and the associated contingency requirements consistent with establishing an essential records list published by Arizona State Library, Archives and Public Records
2. Provides recovery objectives, restoration priorities, and metrics
3. Addresses contingency roles, responsibilities, assigned individuals with contact information
4. Addresses maintaining essential missions and business functions despite an information system disruption, compromise, or failure
5. Addresses eventual, full information systems restoration without deterioration of the security safeguards originally planned and implemented
6. (P) Addresses resumption of essential missions and business functions within a time frame specified by the department CIO and based on mission needs, applicable regulations, Arizona State Library, Archives and Public Records requirements, and applicable contracts and agreements with external departments or other organizations [NIST 800-53 CP-2(3)]
7. (P) Identifies critical information system assets supporting organizational missions and business functions [NIST 800-53 CP-2(8)][HIPAA 164.308(a)(7)(ii)(E)]
8. (P) Includes procedures for obtaining necessary electronic protected health information during an emergency [HIPAA 164.312(a)(2)(ii)]

Manage contingency plan. The department shall [NIST 800-53 CP-2]

1. Distribute the contingency plan to key contingency personnel and organizational elements
2. Coordinate contingency planning activities with security incident handling activities
3. Review the contingency plan annually
4. Revise the contingency plan to address changes to the organization, organization information systems, operational environment or problems encountered during plan implementation, execution, or testing
5. Communicate contingency plan changes to key contingency personnel and organizational elements
6. Protect the contingency plan from unauthorized disclosure and modification

(P) *Contingency plan coordination*: The department shall coordinate the development of the contingency plan for each organization information system with organizational elements responsible for related plans [NIST 800-53 CP-2(1)] [IRS Pub 1075].

Contingency training. The department shall provide contingency training to organization information system users consistent with assigned roles and responsibilities before authorizing access, when required by organization information system changes, and annually thereafter [NIST 800-53 CP-3].

Test contingency plan. The department shall test the contingency plan for the organization information system annually to determine the effectiveness of the plan and the organizational readiness to execute the plan, review the contingency plan test results, and initiate corrective action [NIST 800-53 CP-4][HIPAA 164.308 (a)(7)(ii)(D)].

(P) *Contingency plan test coordination:* The department shall coordinate contingency plan testing for each organization information system with organizational elements responsible for related plans [NIST 800-53 CP-4(1)] [IRS Pub 1075].

(P) *Alternate storage site.* The department shall establish an alternate storage site, including necessary agreements to permit the storage and recovery of information system backup information and ensure that the alternative storage site provides information security safeguards equivalent to those of the primary storage site [NIST 800-53 CP-6].

(P) *Separation from primary storage site*: The alternative storage site shall be separated from the primary storage site to reduce susceptibility to the same hazards [NIST 800-53 CP-6(1)] [IRS Pub 1075].

(P) *Accessibility*: The department shall identify potential accessibility problems to the alternate storage site in the event of an area-wide disruption or disaster and outlines explicit mitigation actions [NIST 800-53 CP-6(3)] [IRS Pub 1075].

(P) *Alternate processing site.* The department shall [NIST 800-53 CP-7] [IRS Pub 1075]

1. Establish an alternate processing site, including necessary agreements to permit the transfer and resumption of organization information system operations for essential missions/business functions with the department's defined time period consistent with recovery time and recovery point objectives when the primary process capabilities are unavailable
2. Ensure that equipment and supplies to transfer and resume operations are available at the alternate site or contracts are in place to support delivery to the site in time to support the department-defined period for transfer/resumption
3. Ensure that the alternate processing site provides information security safeguards equivalent to that of the primary site

   (P) *Separation from primary site*: The department shall identify an alternative processing site that is separated from the primary site to reduce susceptibility to the same threats [NIST 800-53 CP-7(1)] [IRS Pub 1075].

   (P) *Accessibility*: The department shall identify potential accessibility problems to the alternate processing site in the event of an area-wide disruption or disaster and outlines explicit mitigation actions [NIST 800-53 CP-7(2)] [IRS Pub 1075].

   (P) *Priority of service*: The department shall develop alternative processing site agreements that contain priority of service provisions in accordance with the organization's availability requirements [NIST 800-53 CP-7(3)] [IRS Pub 1075].

(P) *Alternate telecommunication site.* The department shall ensure alternate telecommunications services are established, including necessary agreements to permit the resumption of organization information system operations for essential missions and business functions within the department's defined time period when the primary telecommunication capabilities are unavailable at either the primary or alternate processing or storage sites [NIST 800-53 CP-8] [IRS Pub 1075].

(P) *Priority of service provisions*: The department shall ensure primary and alternate telecommunications service agreements are developed that contain priority-of-service provisions in accordance with the department's availability requirements and requests telecommunication service priority for all telecommunications services used for national or state security emergency preparedness in the event that the primary and/or alternate telecommunications services are provided by a common carrier [NIST 800-53 CP-8 (1)] [IRS Pub 1075].

(P) *Single points of failure*: The department shall ensure alternate telecommunications services are obtained, with consideration for reducing the likelihood of sharing a single point of failure with primary telecommunication services [NIST 800-53 CP-8(2)] [IRS Pub 1075].

Information system backup. The department shall [NIST 800-53 CP-9] [HIPAA 164.308(7)(ii)(A)]

1. Conduct backups of user- and system-level information contained in the organization information system, and organization information system documentation, including security-related documentation within the department's defined frequency consistent with recovery time and recovery point objectives

2. Protect the confidentiality, integrity, and availability of the backup information at storage locations

   (P) *Testing for reliability/integrity*: The department shall test backup information at least annually to verify media reliability and information integrity [NIST 800-53 CP-9(1)] [IRS Pub 1075]

Information system recovery and reconstitution. The department shall provide for the recovery and reconstitution of the organization information system to a known state after a disruption, compromise, or failure [NIST 800-53 CP-10]

(P) *Transaction recovery*: The department shall implement organization information systems to perform transaction recovery for any system that is transaction-based [NIST 800-53 CP-10(2)] [IRS Pub 1075]

A.2.4 Policy Example: 8240 Incident Response Planning

Purpose: The purpose of this policy is to increase the ability of the department to rapidly detect incidents, minimize any loss due to destruction, mitigate the weaknesses that were exploited, and restore computing services.

Scope: This policy shall apply to all organization information systems:

- (P)—Policy statements preceded by "(P)" are required for organization information systems categorized as protected.
- (P-PCI)—Policy statements preceded by "(P-PCI)" are required for organization information systems with PCI data (e.g., CHD).

A.2.4.1 Policy Statements   Incident response training. The department shall provide incident response training to organization information system users consistent with assigned roles and responsibilities before authorizing access to the organization information system or performing assigned duties, when required by organization information system changes, and annually thereafter [NIST 800-53 IR-2] [IRS Pub 1075] [PCI DSS 12.9.3].

(P) *Incident response testing.* The department shall test the incident response capability for the organization information system annually using checklists, walk-through, tabletop exercises, simulations, or comprehensive exercises to determine the incident response effectiveness and document the results [NIST 800-53 IR-3] [IRS Pub 1075] [PCI DSS 12.9.2].

(P) *Coordinated testing*: The department shall coordinate incident response testing with department elements responsible for related plans [NIST 800-53 IR-3(2)] [IRS Pub 1075].

Incident handling. The department shall implement an incident handling capability for security incidents that includes [NIST 800-53 IR-4] [IRS Pub 1075] [HIPAA 164.308(a)(6)(ii)] [PCI DSS 12.9.6]

1. Preparation, detection and analysis, containment, eradication, and recovery
2. Incident handling activities with contingency planning activities
3. Incident response procedures, training, and testing/exercises covering lessons learned from ongoing incident handling activities
4. Industry developments
5. Implementation of industry development changes where applicable

    (P) *Automated incident handling processes*: The department shall employ automated mechanisms to support the incident handling process [NIST 800-53 IR-4(1)] [IRS Pub 1075]

    (P) Assign incident handling role: The department shall assign to an individual or team the information security management responsibility of implementing an incident response plan and to be prepared to respond immediately to a system breach [PCI DSS 12.9]

    (P-PCI) 24 × 7 availability: The department shall assign to specific personnel the information security management responsibility of being available on a 24 × 7 basis to respond to alerts [PCI DSS 12.9.3]

(P) *Privacy incident response handling.* The department shall provide an organized and effective response to privacy incidents in accordance with the department privacy incident response plan [NIST 800-53 SE-2].

Incident monitoring. The department shall track and document organization information system security incidents [NIST 800-53 IR-5] [IRS Pub 1075] [HIPAA 164.308(a)(6)(ii)].

(P) *Assign incident monitoring role*: The department shall assign to an individual or team the information security management responsibility of monitoring and analyzing security alerts and information and distributing alerts to appropriate personnel [PCI DSS 12.5.2].

(P) *Incorporate automated alerts*: The department shall implement the system to include alerts from intrusion detection, intrusion prevention, and file integrity monitoring systems [PCI DSS 12.9.5].

Incident reporting. The department shall require personnel to report [NIST 800-53 IR-6] [ARS 41-3507] [IRS Pub 1075] [EO 2008-10] [HIPAA 164.308(a)(6)(ii)] [HIPAA 164.308(a)(1)(ii)(D)] [HIPAA 164.314(a)(2)(i)(C)]

1. Suspected security incidents to the organizational incident response capability within 1 h of knowledge of suspected incident as specified in the Statewide Standard 8240, Incident Response Planning:
   a. (In the event of a security incident) Security incident information to the state CISO
   b. (In the event of a privacy incident) Privacy incident information to the state privacy officer (SPO)

Use of statewide incident handling program: Departments utilizing the statewide incident handling program meet the requirement for reporting of security and privacy incidents that are visible within the program (e.g., part of the monitored systems and logs). However, departments must implement a system to integrate the notification process for security incidents that originate outside of the monitored systems (e.g., employee reported malware, onsite physical threats, and reported loss of laptop) [ARS 41-2507].

(P) *Automated incident reporting*: The department shall employ automated mechanisms to assist in the reporting of security incidents [NIST 800-53 IR-6(1)] [IRS Pub 1075].

Incident response plan. The department shall [NIST 800-53 IR-8] [IRS Pub 1075] [PCI DSS 12.9.1]

1. Develop an incident response plan that
   a. Provides the organization with a roadmap for implementing its incident response capability

    b. Describes the structure and organization of the incident response capability

    c. Provides a high-level approach for how the incident response capability fits into the overall organization

    d. Meets the unique requirements of the organization, which relate to mission, size, structure, and functions

    e. Defines reportable incidents

    f. Provides metrics for measuring the incident response capability within the organization

    g. Defines the resources and management support needed to effectively maintain and manage an incident response capability

    h. (P-PCI) Describes the roles, responsibilities, and communication and contact strategies in the event of a compromise, including notification of the payment brands, specific incident response procedures, business recovery and continuity procedures, data backup processes, analysis of legal requirements for reporting compromises, coverage and responses of all critical system components, and reference or inclusion of incident response procedures from the payment brands [PCI DSS 12.9.1]

    i. Is reviewed and approved by the department information security officer

2. Distribute copies of the incident response plan to incident response personnel and organizational elements

3. Review the incident response plan annually

4. Revise the incident response plan to address system/organizational changes or problems encountered during plan implementation, execution, or testing

5. Communicate incident response plan changes to department incident response personnel and the state CISO and SPO

Incident response assistance. The department shall provide an incident response support resource, integral to the department incident response capability that offers advice and assistance to users of the information system for the handling and reporting of security incidents [NIST 800-53 IR-7] [IRS Pub 1075].

(P) *Automated support for availability of information*: The department shall employ automated mechanisms to increase the availability of incident response-related information and support [NIST 800-53 IR-7(1)] [IRS Pub 1075].

(P) *Privacy incident response plan.* The department shall develop and implement a privacy incident response plan [NIST 800-53 SE-2].

Investigation: The department shall investigate potential privacy incidents upon awareness of unencrypted PII loss [ARS 44-7501].

Notification: The department shall notify affected parties upon breach determination without unreasonable delay [ARS 44-7501].

1. *Non-state-owned PII notification*: For PII not owned by the state, the department shall notify and cooperate with the owner following the discovery of a breach without unreasonable delay [ARS 44-7501].

2. *Notification exceptions*: The department may delay notification if law enforcement determines notification will impede the investigation [ARS 44-7501].

3. *Notification methods*: The department may use telephone, electronic notice, or email as a method of notification [ARS 44-7501].

A.2.5 Policy Example: 8250 Media Protection

Purpose: The purpose of this policy is to increase the ability of the department to ensure the secure storage, transport, and destruction of sensitive information.

Scope: This policy shall apply to all organization information systems:

- (P)—Policy statements preceded by "(P)" are required for organization information systems categorized as protected.
- (P-PHI)—Policy statements preceded by "(P-PHI)" are required for organization information systems with protected healthcare information.

A.2.5.1 Policy Statements Media access. The department shall restrict access to digital and nondigital media to authorized individuals [NIST 800-53 MP-2] [HIPAA 164.308(a)(3)(ii)(A)] [PCI DSS 9.9] [IRS Pub 1075].

(P) *Media marking.* The department shall mark, in accordance with department policies and procedures, information system digital and nondigital media containing confidential information indicating the distribution limitations, handling caveats, and applicable security markings (if any) of the information, as well as exempt removable digital media from marking as long as the exempted items remain with a controlled environment [NIST 800-53 MP-3] [PCI DSS 9.7.1] [IRS Pub 1075].

(P) *Media storage.* The department shall physically control and securely store digital and nondigital media containing confidential information within controlled areas [NIST 800-53 MP-4] [ARS 39-101] [PCI DSS 9.6] [PCI DSS 9.9] [IRS Pub 1075].

(P) *Media inventories.* The department shall maintain inventory logs of all digital media containing confidential information and conduct inventories annually [PCI DSS 9.9.1].

(P) *Media transport.* The department shall protect and control digital and nondigital media containing confidential information during transport outside controlled areas [NIST 800-53 MP-5] [PCI DSS 9.7] [IRS Pub 1075].

(P) *Cryptographic protection*: The department shall employ cryptographic mechanisms to protect the confidentiality and integrity of information stored on digital media during transport outside controlled areas. Cryptographic mechanisms must comply with System and Communication Protection Standard S8350 [NIST 800-53 MP-5(4)] [HIPAA 164.312(c)(2)] [IRS Pub 1075].

(P) *Secure delivery*: The department shall send confidential digital and nondigital media by secured courier or other delivery method [PCI DSS 9.7.2].

(P-PHI) *Record of movement*: The department shall maintain a record, including the person(s) responsible, of the movements of hardware and digital media [HIPAA 164.310(d)(2)(iii)].

(P) *Data backup*: The department shall create a retrievable, exact copy of confidential data, when needed before movement of equipment [HIPAA 164.310(d)(2)(iv)].

(P) *Backup storage*: The department shall store digital media backups in a secure location and review the location's security, at least annually [PCI DSS 9.5].

(P) *Management approval*: The department shall ensure management approves any media that is moved from a controlled area [PCI DSS 9.8].

Media sanitization: The department shall sanitize digital and nondigital information system media containing confidential information prior to disposal, release of organizational control, or release for reuse using defined sanitization techniques and procedures in accordance with the Media Protection Standard S8250 [NIST 800-53 MP-6] [HIPAA 164.310(d)(2)(i)] [HIPAA 164.310(d)(2)(ii)] [IRS Pub 1075].

Media use: The department shall restrict the use of [department-specified type of digital media] on [department-specified organization information systems and/or system components] [NIST 800-53 MP-7] [IRS Pub 1075].

(P) *Department restrictions*: The department shall employ PSPs on the use of removable media in the department's information systems [NIST 800-53 MP-7(1)] [HIPAA 164.310(d)(1)].

(P) *Prohibition of use without known owner*: The department shall prohibit the use of removable media in the department's information systems when the media has no identifiable owner [NIST 800-53 MP-7(2)] [IRS Pub 1075].

A.2.6 Policy Example: 8260 Physical Security Protections

Purpose: The purpose of this policy is to protect organization information systems and assets through limiting and controlling physical access and implementing controls to protect the environment in which organization information systems and assets are housed.

Scope: This policy shall apply to all organization information systems:

- (P)—Policy statements preceded by "(P)" are required for organization information systems categorized as protected.

- (P-PCI)—Policy statements preceded by "(P-PCI)" are required for organization information systems with PCI data (e.g., CHD).

A.2.6.1 Policy Statements *Physical access authorizations*: The department shall [NIST 800-53 PE-2] [IRS Pub 1075] [HIPAA 164.310 (a)(2)(iii)]

1. Develop and maintain a list of individuals with authorized access to controlled areas or facilities where the organization information system resides
2. Issue authorization credentials
3. Review and approve the access list and authorization credentials quarterly
4. Remove individuals from the access list when access is no longer required

Standard physical access control: The department shall [NIST 800-53 PE-3] [IRS Pub 1075] [AAC 2-10] [HIPAA 164.310(a)(1), (a)(2)(ii)]

1. Enforce physical access authorization at designated entry/exit points to the facility where the organization information system resides [PCI 9.1]
2. Verify individual access authorizations before granting access to the facility [PCI 9.1, 9.3.1]
3. Control ingress/egress to the facility using keys, locks, combinations, card readers, and/or guards
4. (P-PCI) Provide cameras, monitoring by guards, or isolating selected organization information system components to control access to areas within the facility officially designated as publically accessible [PCI 9.1.1]

Protected physical access control. For all protected organization information systems and the server components of standard organization information systems for which additional physical protections apply, the department shall [NIST 800-53 PE-3] [IRS Pub 1075] [AAC 2-10] [HIPAA 164.310(a)(1), (a)(2)(ii)]

1. (P) Develop procedures to easily distinguish between onsite personnel and visitors [PCI 9.2]

2. (P) Give visitors a physical token that expires and that identifies the visitors as onsite personnel and ensure the visitor surrenders the physical token before leaving the facility or at the date of expiration [PCI 9.3.2, 9.3.3]
3. Escort visitors and monitors visitor activity within controlled areas
4. Secure keys, combinations, and other physical access devices
5. Inventory keys and other physical access devices every quarter; keys and other physical access devices assigned to visitors are inventoried every day
6. Change combinations annually and combinations and keys when keys are lost, combinations are compromised, or individuals are transferred or separated

Monitoring physical access: The department shall [NIST 800-53 PE-6] [IRS Pub 1075]

1. Monitor physical access to the organization information system to detect and respond to physical security incidents
2. (P) Review physical access logs weekly and, upon occurrence of potential indications of events [PCI 9.1.1]
3. (P) Coordinate results of reviews and investigations with the organizational incident response capability
4. (P) Store physical access monitoring data for at least 3 months [PCI 9.1.1]

   (P) *Intrusion alarms/surveillance equipment*: The department shall monitor real-time physical intrusion alarms and surveillance equipment [NIST 800-53 PE-6(1)] [IRS Pub 1075]

Visitor control records: The department shall

1. Maintain visitor access records to the controlled areas or facilities where the information system resides
2. Review visitor access records monthly [NIST 800-53 PE-8]
3. Maintain a visitor log that includes the visitor's name, the firm represented, and the onsite personnel authorizing physical access
4. The logs shall be retained for a minimum of 3 months [PCI 9.4]

(P) *Access control*: The department shall implement the following physical access controls:

   (P) *Transmission medium*: The department shall control physical access to organization information system distribution and transmission lines within the department's facilities using locked wiring closets; disconnected or locked spare jacks; and/or protection of cabling by conduit or cable trays [NIST 800-53 PE-4] [IRS Pub 1075].

   (P) *Workstations*: The department shall implement physical safeguards for all workstations that access sensitive information to restrict access to authorized users [HIPAA 164.310(b), 164.310(c)].

   (P) *Output devices*: The department shall control physical access to organization information system output devices to prevent unauthorized individuals from obtaining output [NIST 800-53 PE-5] [IRS Pub 1075].

   (P-PCI) *Network jacks and devices*: The department shall restrict physical access to publically accessible network jacks, wireless access points, gateways, handheld devices, networking/communications hardware, and telecommunication lines [PCI 9.1.2].

   (P) *Power equipment and cabling*: The department shall protect power equipment and power cabling for the organization information system from damage and destruction [NIST 800-53 PE-9].

(P) *Power*. The department shall implement the following physical controls for power:

   (P) *Emergency shutoff*: The department shall [NIST 800-53 PE-10]
      1. Provide the capability of shutting off power to the organization information system or individual system components in emergency situations
      2. Place emergency shutoff switches or devices in data centers, server rooms, and computer rooms to facilitate safe and easy access for personnel

3. Protect emergency power shutoff capability from unau-
    thorized activation

(P) *Emergency power*: The department shall provide a short-term
    uninterruptable power supply to facilitate an orderly shutdown
    of the information system or a transition of the information
    system to long-term alternate power in the event of a primary
    power source loss [NIST 800-53 PE-11].

Emergency lighting: The department shall employ and maintain
automatic emergency lighting for the organization information system that activates in the event of a power outage or disruption and
that covers emergency exits and evacuation routes within the facility
[NIST 800-53 PE-12].

Fire protection: The department shall employ and maintain fire
suppression and detection devices/systems for the organization information system that are supported by an independent energy source
[NIST 800-53 PE-13].

(P) *Detection devices*: The department shall employ fire detection
    devices/systems for the organization information system that
    activate automatically and notify the department and emer-
    gency responders in the event of a fire [NIST 800-53 PE-13(1)].
(P) *Suppression devices*: The department shall employ fire sup-
    pression devices/systems for the organization information
    system that provides automatic notification of any activation
    to the department and emergency responders [NIST 800-53
    PE-13(2)].
(P) *Inspections*: The department shall ensure the facility under-
    goes annual inspections by authorized and qualified inspec-
    tors and resolves identified deficiencies within 30 days [NIST
    800-53 PE-13(3)].

Temperature and humidity controls. The department shall maintain
defined temperature and humidity levels within the facility where the
organization information system resides at data centers, server rooms
and computer rooms, and monitors temperature and humidity levels
daily [NIST 800-53 PE-14].

Water damage protection: The department shall protect organization
information systems from damage resulting from water leakage by

providing master shutoff or isolation valves that are accessible, working properly, and known to key personnel [NIST 800-53 PE-15].

Delivery and removal: The department shall authorize, monitor, and control organization information systems components entering and exiting the facility and maintain records of those items [NIST 800-53 PE-16].

(P) *Alternate work site:* The department shall [NIST 800-53 PE-17]

1. Define and employ minimum security controls at alternate work sites
2. Assess, as feasible, the effectiveness of security controls at alternate work sites
3. Provide a means for employees to communicate with organization information security personnel in case of security incidents or problems

A.2.7 Policy Example: 8270 Personnel Security Controls

Purpose: The purpose of this policy is to increase the ability of the department to protect organization information systems and assets containing sensitive data through personnel security controls.

Scope: This policy shall apply to all organization information systems:

- (P)—Policy statements preceded by "(P)" are required for organization information systems categorized as protected.

A.2.7.1 Policy Statements   *Position categorization:* The department shall

1. Assign a sensitivity designation (e.g., sensitive and nonsensitive) to all positions
2. Establish screening criteria for individuals filling those positions
3. Review and revise position sensitivity designations annually. Sensitivity designations are based on the individual's exposure to sensitive system information and/or administrative privileges to organization information systems. Examples of sensitive positions include [NIST 800-53 PS-02] [IRS Pub 1075]
   a. Firewall administrator
   b. Members of the incident response team
   c. Those with vulnerability scanning duties

Position definition: The department shall define information security responsibilities for all personnel [HIPAA(a)(3)(ii)(A), (a)(3)(ii)(B)—Addressable] [PCI 12.4]. Specifically, the following information security responsibilities:

1. Individual or team responsible for establishing, documenting, and distributing security policies and procedures [PCI 12.5.1]
2. Individual or team responsible for monitoring and analyzing security alerts and information, and distributing to appropriate employees and contractors [PCI 12.5.2]
3. Individual or team responsible for establishing, documenting, and distributing security incident response and escalation procedures to ensure timely and effective handling of all situations [PCI 12.5.3]
4. Individual or team responsible for administering user accounts, including additions, deletions, and modifications [PCI 12.5.4]
5. Individual or team responsible for monitoring and controlling all access to data [PCI 12.5.5]

Personnel screening: The department shall screen individuals holding positions designated as sensitive prior to hiring or contracting; and rescreens individuals according to rescreening every 3 years [NIST 800-53 PS-03] [IRS Pub 1075] [PCI 12.7].

Personnel separation: Upon separation of individual employment, the department shall [NIST 800-53 PS-04] [HIPAA(a)(3)(ii)(C)]

1. Terminate organization information system access within 24 h
2. Conduct exit interviews, if employee is available for interview
3. Retrieve all security-related organization information system-related property
4. Retain access to organization information system accounts formerly controlled by separated individual
5. Allow the separated individual access to authorized services such as benefits, reimbursement, and retirement information, according to department or state policies

Personnel transfer: The department shall [NIST 800-53 PS-05] [IRS Pub 1075]

1. Review logical and physical access authorization to organization information systems/facilities when personnel are reassigned or transferred to other positions within the organization and initiates returning old and reissuing new keys, identification cards, and building passes
2. Close previous information system accounts and establish new accounts
3. Change organization information system access authorizations
4. Provide access to official records to which the employee had access at the previous work location and in the previous organization information system accounts within 24 h
5. The department may extend limited access for special purposes on an exception basis

Access agreements: The department shall ensure that individuals requiring access to organization information systems acknowledge and accept appropriate access agreement prior to being granted access and reviews/updates the access agreements annually [NIST 800-53 PS-06] [IRS Pub 1075] [PCI 12.3].

Third-party personnel security. The department shall [NIST 800-53 PS-07] [IRS Pub 1075] [HIPAA 164.314(a)(1)]

1. Establish personnel security requirements, including security roles and responsibilities for third-party providers
2. Document personnel security requirements
3. Monitor provider compliance

Third-party contracts: The department shall ensure that third-party contractors specify the third party will [HIPAA 164.314(a)(2)(i)]

1. Comply with the applicable security requirements
2. Ensure that any subcontractors who create, receive, maintain, or transmit sensitive information on behalf of the third-party agree to comply with applicable requirements
3. Report to the department any security incident of which it becomes aware, including breaches of unsecured sensitive information

Personnel sanctions: The department shall employ a formal sanctions process for personnel failing to comply with established organization information security and privacy PSPs and document the sanctions applied [NIST 800-53 PS-08] [IRS Pub 1075] [HIPAA 164.308(a)(1)(ii)(C)] [HIPAA 164.530(e)(1),(2)].

A.2.8 Policy Example: 8280 Acceptable Use

Purpose: The purpose of this policy is to outline the acceptable use of organization information system assets to reduce the risks to organization information systems due to disclosure, modification, or disruption, whether intentional or accidental.

Scope: This policy shall apply to all users of organization information systems.

A.2.8.1 Policy Statements Access agreements: The department director shall ensure that individuals requiring access to organizational information and organization information systems acknowledge and accept appropriate access agreements (prior to being granted access) and shall review and, if necessary, update the access agreements annually [NIST 800-53 PS-6] [PCI DSS 12.3].

> *Assign responsibility to provide policy*: The department director shall assign responsibility to a department, role, or named individual to provide acceptable use and other related information security policies to employees and contractors.
> *Assign responsibility to keep records*: The department director shall assign responsibility to a department, role, or named individual to keep records of distributed, acknowledged, and accepted acceptable use policies for employees and contractors.

Access agreement contents: The access agreements shall contain the following policy sections and statements:

> *Expected behaviors*: The following behaviors shall be required:
> > *Practice safe computing*: Those accessing organization information systems shall use caution and exercise good security practices to ensure the protection of organization information systems and data, including, but not limited to

1. *Opening attachments or links*: Use caution when opening email attachments or following hypertext links received from unknown senders.
2. *Keep passwords secure:* Select strong passwords, do not write them down, change them frequently, and do not share them with anyone.
3. *Keep desk and workstation secure*: Use available operating system functions to lock the workstation when away from the desk. At the end of the day, log out of the computer, but leave the equipment powered on.
4. *Challenge unauthorized personnel*: Assist in enforcing physical access controls by challenging unauthorized personnel who may not be following procedures for visitor sign-in, appropriate badge use, escort control, and/or entry.
5. *Report security or privacy weaknesses or violations*: Report any weaknesses in computer security or data privacy, suspicious behavior of others, and any incidents of possible misuse or violation of this policy to the proper authorities.
6. *Wear issued badges*: All employees and contractors are required to wear their organization-issued identification (ID) badges, while in the building, at all times.

Protect confidential information: Confidential information shall be protected in accordance with applicable statutes, rules, and PSPs. Those accessing organization information systems shall protect confidential information in accordance with the Policy 8110, Data Classification and Handling, specifically, the following:

Marking of confidential information: All nonpublic data must be marked (labeled) as confidential. Unlabeled data are assumed to be public.

Unencrypted confidential information: Confidential information sent over email or other electronic messaging without adequate encryption shall be prohibited (even to an authorized user).

Storage of confidential information: Confidential information must be stored in accordance with the Policy 8250, Media Protection.

Electronic transmission of confidential information: Confidential information that are transmitted outside of the organization information system or on any medium that can be accessed by authorized users shall be encrypted through link or end-to-end encryption with an encryption algorithm and key length that meets the Standard 8350, System and Communication Protection.

Prohibited behaviors: The following behaviors shall be prohibited:

1. *Computer tampering*: Unauthorized access, interception, modification, or destruction of any computer, computer system, organization information system, computer programs, or data [ARS 13-2316.1-2].

2. *Use of unauthorized computing equipment*: Installation or connections of any computing equipment not provided or authorized by management to organization information systems.

3. *Use of unauthorized software*: Installation or use of any unauthorized software, including but not limited to security testing, monitoring, encryption, or "hacking" software on organization computing resources [NIST 800 53 CM-11].

4. *Unauthorized use of software or services*: Use of peer-to-peer file sharing technology used for the unauthorized distribution, display, performance, or reproduction of copyrighted work [NIST 800 53 CM-10].

5. *Introduction of malware*: Knowingly introducing a computer contaminant into any computer, computer system, or organization information system [ARS 13-2316.3].

6. *System disruption*: Recklessly disrupting or causing the disruption of a computer, computer system, or organization information system [ARS 13-2316.4].

7. *Circumvention of security controls*: Disabling software, modifying configurations, or otherwise circumventing security controls [ARS 13-2316]. Tampering with

physical security measures (e.g., locks and cameras) is also prohibited.

8. *False identity*: Falsifying identification information or routing information so as to obscure the origins or the identity of the sender, or using or assuming any information system or application identification other than your own.

Unauthorized inappropriate or unlawful material: The unauthorized storage, transmission, or viewing of any pornography or other offensive, intimidating, hostile, or otherwise illegal material is forbidden. Except to the extent required in conjunction with a bona fide organization-approved research project or other organization-approved undertaking, an employee of an organization shall not knowingly use organization-owned or organization-leased computer equipment to access, download, print, or store any information infrastructure files or services that depict nudity, sexual activity, sexual excitement, or ultimate sex acts [ARS 38-448] [ARS 13-2316.5].

Unauthorized use of electronic messaging: The following use of electronic messaging shall be prohibited:

1. *Spam:* Sending of unsolicited commercial emails/electronic messages in bulk (identical content to multiple recipients)

2. *Chain letters*: Creating or forwarding chain letters or pyramid schemes

3. *Unprofessional communications*: Unprofessional or un-businesslike in appearance or content

4. *Alter message content*: Modification or deletion of email/electronic messages originating from another person or computer with the intent to deceive

5. *False identity*: Falsifying email/electronic message headers or routing information so as to obscure the origins of the email/electronic message or the identity of the sender, also known as spoofing

6. *Mask identity*: Unauthorized use of anonymous addresses for sending and receiving email/electronic messages

7. *Auto-forward to external accounts:* Automatically forwarding email/electronic messages sent to a department account to an external email/electronic messages without authorization

8. *Nonorganization email accounts:* Unauthorized use of a nonorganization email account for organization business

9. *Unencrypted confidential information:* Confidential information sent over email or other electronic messaging without adequate encryption (even to an authorized user)

10. *Misrepresentation of department:* Presenting viewpoints or positions not held by the department as those of the department or attributing them to the department

Personal use of department information systems: Personal use of organization technology assets/information systems shall be limited to occasional use during break periods provided the use does not interfere with organization information systems or services.

Violation of intellectual property laws: Unauthorized receipt, use, or distribution of unlicensed software, copyrighted materials, or communications of proprietary information or trade secrets.

Unauthorized access of confidential information: Unauthorized access of information that has been classified as confidential could cause harm to the state and/or the citizens of the state. The confidentiality of information is protected by law. The unauthorized access of any confidential information is prohibited [ARS 13-2316.07].

Unauthorized release of confidential information: Disclosure of information that has been classified as confidential could cause harm to the state and/or the citizens of the state. The confidentiality of information is protected by law. The unauthorized release or disclosure of any confidential information is prohibited [ARS 36-342] [ARS 36-666] [ARS 41-151.12] [ARS 41-1750.01].

Unauthorized posting of department documents: Unauthorized posting of organization draft or final organization documents is prohibited.

Notifications and acknowledgments: The following notifications and acknowledgments shall be used to inform those granted access to organizational information and/or organization information systems of steps the department may take to ensure the security of organization information systems:

User responsibility acknowledgment: All users review and acknowledge their understanding of this policy and other related information security policies on an annual basis [PCI DSS 12.6.2].

Assets and intellectual property: All organization information system assets remain the sole property of the State of Arizona. Any data or intellectual property created by the user, including voicemail and electronic messages, shall remain the property of the State of Arizona and shall not be removed, copied, or shared with any person or entity except as part of the user's normal job responsibilities.

Monitoring: The department shall inform all users that it reserves the right to monitor all activities that occur on its organization information systems or to access any data residing on its systems or assets at any time without further notice. The department shall retain the right to override an individual's passwords and/or codes to facilitate access by the department.

Potential blocking of inappropriate content: The department may block access to web content it deems as inappropriate or filter email destined for your mailbox.

Incomplete blocking of inappropriate content: The department shall not be responsible for material viewed or downloaded by users from the Internet or messages delivered to a user's mailbox. Users are cautioned that many Internet pages and emails include offensive, sexually explicit, and inappropriate material. Even though the department intends to filter and block inappropriate content and messages, it is not possible to always avoid contact with offensive content on the Internet or in your email. If such an action occurs, users are expected to delete the offensive material, leave the offensive site, and contact the department security.

Records retention: Files, emails, attachments, and other records are retained, preserved, and/or disposed of in accordance with department records retention policies and in full accordance with the State Library Records Retention Schedule, Electronic Communication Records.

No expectation of privacy: Users shall have no expectation of privacy for any communication or data created, stored, sent, or received on organization information systems and assets.

User acknowledgment: By using organization information systems, users shall acknowledge that they explicitly consent to the monitoring of such use and the right of the department to conduct such monitoring.

Virtual office agreement: The department shall ensure that individuals utilizing computing equipment outside of designated work environments (e.g., virtual offices, working from home, and telework centers) to access organization information systems as a trusted user acknowledge and accept appropriate access agreements prior to being granted access and shall review, and if necessary, update agreements annually.

Assign responsibility to provide policy: The department shall assign responsibility to a department, role, or named individual to provide acceptable use and other related information security policies to employees and contractors.

Assign responsibility to keep records: The department shall assign responsibility to a department, role, or named individual to keep records of distributed, acknowledged, and accepted acceptable use policies for employees and contractors.

Virtual office access agreement contents: The virtual office access agreements shall contain the following additional policy sections and statements:

(P) *Allowable computing devices*: An individual utilizing computing equipment outside of designated work environments (e.g., virtual offices, working from home, and telework centers) to access organization information systems as a trusted user providing and storing confidential information shall ensure

1. The computing equipment is issued to the individual by the organization for the purposes of connecting to an organization information system, or
2. The computing equipment is owned or otherwise under the control of the individual such that the individual may ensure minimum physical and logical protections are in place

(P) *Physical protection of computing devices*: An individual utilizing computing equipment outside of designated work environments (e.g., virtual offices, working from home, and telework centers) to access organization information systems as a trusted user providing and storing confidential information shall ensure that computer equipment is

1. Physically protected from unauthorized use and removal.
2. Limited to the use of the authorized virtual office user. Use of the computer equipment by anyone else (e.g., family members and roommates) is strictly forbidden.

(P) *Logical protection of computing devices*: An individual utilizing computing equipment outside of designated work environments (e.g., virtual offices, working from home, and telework centers) to access organization information systems as a trusted user providing and storing confidential information shall ensure that computer equipment has the following logical security controls:

1. *Username and passwords*: Identification and authentication controls consistent with Policy 8340, Identification and Authentication.
2. *Antivirus*: Malicious code protection consistent with Policy 8220, System Security Maintenance, with the exception of central management of malicious code protection.
3. *Personal firewalls*: Personal firewalls consistent with Policy 8320, Access Control.
4. *Device encryption*: Full device encryption consistent with the Access Control Policy.

5. *Security patches*: Install security-relevant software and firmware updates consistent with Policy 8220, System Security Maintenance.

Remote access: Virtual office users may access the organization information system only by approved access methods.

User-based technologies: The department shall ensure that individuals utilizing user-based technologies (e.g., smart phones and tablet computers) to access organization information systems as a trusted user acknowledge and accept appropriate access agreements (prior to being granted access), and shall review, and if necessary, update agreements annually.

Assign responsibility to provide policy: The department shall assign responsibility to a department, role, or named individual to provide user-technology standards, acceptable use, and other related information security policies to employees and contractors.

Assign responsibility to keep records: The department shall assign responsibility to a department, role, or named individual to keep records of distributed, acknowledged, and accepted acceptable use policies for employees and contractors.

User-based technology agreement contents: The user-based technology access agreements shall be developed by the department and contains department-defined security controls. Statewide Standard 8220, System Security Maintenance provides guidance to department for minimum recommended user-based technology controls.

Consequences for noncompliance: Users of organization information systems who fail to comply with established information security and privacy policies and procedures may be subject to sanctions, including referral to a law enforcement organization for appropriate action [NIST 80053 PS-8] [HIPAA 164.308(a)(1)(ii)(C)] [HIPAA 164.530(e)(1),(2)].

Department employees: State Personnel System (SPS) Rule R2-5A-501, Standards of Conduct, requires that all employees comply with federal and state laws and rules, statewide policies, and employee handbook and organization policy and directives. As provided by SPS Rule R2-5A-501(C), an employee who fails to comply with standards of conduct requirements may be disciplined or separated from state employment.

Department contractors: Department contractors violating federal and state laws and rules, statewide policies, and organization policy and directives may result in, but not be limited to, immediate credential revocation, terminations of permissions for access to data systems and physical locations, and barring entry or access permanently. Vendors providing services under a contract are subject to vendor performance reports, and any contract terms and warranties, including potential damages.

A.3 Information Security Technical Policy Examples

Based on the Arizona Policy and Standards project, five policies were created to address the operations of the information security program. Technical policies cover the information security controls within the information systems such as account management, access control, and system security audit.

A.3.1 Policy Example: 8310 Account Management

Purpose: The purpose of this policy is to establish the baseline controls for the administration of organization information system accounts.

   Scope: This policy shall apply to all organization information systems:

- (P)—Policy statements preceded by "(P)" are required for organization information systems categorized as protected.

A.3.1.1 Policy Statements (P) *Automated account management*: The department shall employ automated mechanisms to support the management of information system accounts [NIST 800-53 AC-2(1)] [IRS Pub 1075] [PCI DSS 7.1.4].

   (P) *Develop account management operational procedures*: The department shall develop daily operational security procedures that are consistent with requirements in this specification [PCI DSS 12.2].

Identify account types: The department shall identify the types of organization information system accounts to support organizational missions/business functions (e.g., individual, guest, emergency access, developer, maintenance, and administration) [NIST 800-53 AC-2a] [HIPAA 164.312 (a)(2)(iii)—Addressable] [PCI DSS 7.2.2].

> *Establish group and role-based accounts*: The department shall establish conditions for group and role membership [NIST 800-53 AC-2c] [PCI DSS 7.1.2] [PCI DSS 7.2.2].
>
> *Account specification*: The department shall specify authorized users of the organization information system, group and role membership, and access authorizations (i.e., privileges) and other attributes for each account [NIST 800-53 AC-2d].
>
> (P) *Privileged accounts*: The department shall restrict privileged accounts (e.g., super user accounts) on the organization information system to administrative roles [NIST 800-53 AC-6(5)] [IRS Pub 1075].
>
> (P) *Separation of duties*: The department shall separate department-defined duties; documents separation of duties of individuals; and defines organization information system access authorizations to support separation of duties [NIST 800-53 AC-5] [IRS Pub 1075].

Assign account managers: The department shall assign account managers for organization information system accounts [NIST 800-53 AC-2b].

Account approval: The department shall require documented approvals by authorized department staff for requests to create, modify, and enable organization information system accounts [NIST 800-53 AC-2e-f] [PCI DSS 7.1.3].

> (P) *Automated audit actions*: The department shall ensure the organization information system automatically audits account creation, modification, enabling, disabling, and removal actions and notifies, as required department-defined personnel or roles [NIST 800-53 AC-2(4)] [IRS Pub 1075].

Account monitoring: The department shall authorize and monitor the use of organization information system accounts [NIST 800-53 AC-2g].

(P) *Vendor account monitoring*: The department shall enable accounts used by vendors for remote access only during the time period needed and monitors the vendor remote access accounts when in use [PCI DSS 8.5.6].

Account removal: The department shall notify account managers when accounts are no longer required; users are separated or transferred; and individual information system usage or need-to-know changes [NIST 800-53 AC-2h] [PCI DSS 8.5.4].

(P) *Immediate removal of separated users:* The department shall immediately revoke access for any separated users [PCI DSS 8.5.4].

(P) *Automatic removal of temporary accounts*: The organization information system automatically removes or disables temporary and emergency accounts after a department-defined time [NIST 800-53 AC-2(2)] [IRS Pub 1075].

(P) *Disable inactive accounts*: The department shall ensure the organization information system automatically disables inactive accounts after department-defined time period. For organization information systems containing CHD, the time period must be no more than 90 days [NIST 800-53 AC-2(3)] [IRS Pub 1075] [PCI DSS 8.5.5].

Access authorization: The department shall authorize access to the organization information system based on a valid access authorization, intended system usage, and other attributes as required by the organization or associated mission functions [NIST 800-53 AC-2f,i] [HIPAA 164.308 (4)(ii)(B)—Addressable].

(P) *Default "deny-all" setting*: The department shall ensure the organization information system access control system is set to "deny all" unless specifically allowed [PCI DSS 7.2.3].

(P) *Restrict direct database access*: The department shall ensure the organization information system authenticates all access to any database containing confidential information and restricts direct access or queries to databases to database administrators [PCI DSS 8.5.16].

Accounts rights review: The department shall review accounts for compliance with account management requirements annually [NIST 800-53 AC-2j] [HIPAA 164.308 (4)(ii)(C)—Addressable].

Reissues account credentials: The department shall establish a process for reissuing shared/group account credentials (if deployed) when individuals are removed from the group [NIST 800-53 AC-2k].

A.3.2 Policy Example: 8320 Access Control

Purpose: The purpose of this policy is to define the correct use and management of logical access controls for the protection of organization information systems and assets.

Scope: This policy shall apply to all organization information systems:

- (P)—Policy statements preceded by "(P)" are required for organization information systems categorized as protected.

A.3.2.1 Policy Statements Access enforcement: The department shall ensure the organization information system enforces approved authorizations for logical access to information and system resources in accordance with applicable control policies (e.g., identity-based policies and role-based policies) [NIST 800-53 AC-3] [HIPAA 164.308(a)(3) (ii)(A)—Addressable, 164.308 (a)(4)(ii)(B) & (C)—Addressable].

(P) *Assign responsibility*: The department shall assign to an individual or team the security management responsibility of monitoring and controlling all access to confidential data [PCI DSS 12.5.5].

(P) *Develop access control operational procedures:* The department shall develop daily operational security procedures that are consistent with requirements in this specification [PCI DSS 12.2].

(P) *Information flow enforcement*: The department shall ensure the organization information system enforces approved authorizations for controlling the flow of information within the system and between interconnected systems based on department-defined information flow control policies, including Statewide Policy Framework 8350, Systems and Communications Protections. These policies prohibit direct public access between the Internet and any system component in the protected organization information system [NIST 800-53 AC-4] [IRS Pub 1075] [PCI DSS 1.3].

(P) *Perimeter firewalls for wireless networks*: The department shall install perimeter firewalls between any wireless network and the protected organization information system, and configures these firewalls to deny or control (if such traffic is necessary for business purposes) any traffic from the wireless environment into the protected organization information system [PCI DSS 1.2.3].

(P) *Personal firewalls*: The department shall require personal firewall software on any mobile device and/or employee-owned computers with direct connectivity to the Internet that is used to access the department's network [PCI DSS 1.4].

(P) *Least privilege*: The department shall employ the concept of least privilege, allowing only authorized accesses for users (and processes acting on behalf of users), which are necessary to accomplish assigned tasks in accordance with organizational missions and business functions [NIST 800-53 AC-6] [IRS Pub 1075] [PCI DSS 7.1].

(P) *Organizational isolation*: The department shall implement policies and procedures that protect confidential information from unauthorized access by other (e.g., larger department of which the department is a part of) organizations [HIPAA 164.308 (a)(4)(ii)(A)].

(P) *Privileged accounts*: The department shall restrict access rights to privileged user accounts to least privileges necessary to perform job responsibilities [PCI 7.1.1].

(P) *Job classification*: The department shall restrict access rights based on individual personnel's job classification and function [PCI DSS 7.1.2].

(P) *Authorize access to security functions*: The department shall explicitly authorize access to the following security functions and security-relevant information [NIST 800-53 AC-6(1)] [IRS Pub 1075]:

1. Establishing system accounts
2. Configuring access authorizations
3. Setting events to be audited

4. Setting intrusion detection parameters

5. Filtering rules for routers and firewalls

6. Cryptographic key-management information

7. Configuration parameters for security services

(P) *Nonprivileged access for nonsecurity functions*: The department shall require that users of organization information system accounts, or roles, with access to security functions (e.g., privileged users), use nonprivileged accounts or roles, when accessing nonsecurity functions [NIST 800-53 AC-6(2)] [IRS Pub 1075].

(P) *Auditing of privileged functions*: The department shall include execution of privileged functions in the events to be audited by the organization information system [NIST 800-53 AC-6(9)].

(P) *Prohibit nonprivileged users from executing privileged functions*: The department shall ensure the organization information system prevents nonprivileged users from executing privileged functions to include disabling, circumventing, or altering implemented security safeguards/countermeasures [NIST 800-53 AC-6(10)] [IRS Pub 1075].

Unsuccessful logon attempts: The department shall ensure the organization information system enforces a department-specified limit of consecutive invalid logon attempts by a user; and automatically locks the account/node for a department-specified period of time or locks the account/node until released by an administrator when the maximum number of unsuccessful attempts is exceeded, consistent with the Statewide Access Control Standard 8320 [NIST 800-53 AC-7] [PCI DSS 8.5.13].

System use notification: The department shall ensure the organization information system [NIST 800-53 AC-8]:

Displays to users a department-defined notification banner before granting access to the system that provides privacy and security notices consistent with applicable federal laws, state laws, executive orders, directives, policies, regulations, standards, and guidance and shall state the following:

1. Users are accessing an organization information system owned by the State of Arizona

2. Department information system usage may be monitored, recorded, and subject to audit

3. Unauthorized use of the organization information system is prohibited and subject to criminal and civil penalties

4. Use of the organization information system indicates consents to monitoring and recording

5. Retains the notification banner on the screen until users acknowledge the usage conditions and take explicit actions to log on to or further access the organization information system

   • For publicly accessible systems; the organization information system shall also

   • Display to users the system use organization information before granting further access

   • Display to users references, if any, to monitoring, recording, or auditing that are consistent with privacy accommodations for such systems that generally prohibit those activities

6. Include in the notice given to public users of the organization information system, a description of the authorized uses of the system

(P) *Session lock:* The department shall ensure the organization information system prevents further access to the system by initiating a department-specified limit of time inactivity or upon receiving a request from a user; and retains the session lock for a department-specified limit of time or until the user reestablishes access using established identification and authentication procedures. If the user does not reestablish access within a department-specified limit of time, the session is dropped [NIST 800-53 AC-11] [IRS Pub 1075] [HIPAA 164.312 (a)(2)(iii)] [PCI DSS 8.5.14, 8.5.15].

Permitted actions without identification or authentication: The department shall identify user actions that can be performed on the organization information system without identification or authentication consistent with department missions; and documents and provides support rationale in the security plan for the organization information system, user actions not requiring identification or authentication [NIST 800-53 AC-14].

Remote access: The department shall establish usage restrictions, configuration/connection requirements, and implementation guidance for each type of remote access allowed; and authorizes remote access to the organization information system prior to allowing such connections [NIST 800-53 AC-17].

(P) *Automated monitoring/control*: The department shall ensure the organization information system monitors and controls remote access methods (e.g., detection of cyber attacks such as false logins and denial of service attacks and compliance with remote access policies such as strength of encryption) [NIST 800-53 AC-17(1)] [IRS Pub 1075].

(P) *Security using encryption*: The department shall ensure the organization information system implements cryptographic mechanisms to protect the confidentiality and integrity of remote access sessions, consistent with the Statewide Standard 8350 System and Communication Protection [NIST 800-53 AC-17(2)] [IRS Pub 1075] [PCI DSS 2.3, 4.1].

(P) *Managed access control points:* The department shall ensure the organization information system routes all remote accesses through a limited number of managed network access control points [NIST 800-53 AC-17(3)] [IRS Pub 1075].

(P) *Privileged access commands*: The department shall authorize the execution of privileged commands and access to security-relevant information using remote access only for department-defined needs, and documents the rationale for such access in the security plan for the organization information system [NIST 800-53 AC-17(4)] [IRS Pub 1075].

Wireless access: The department shall establish usage restrictions, configuration/connection requirements, and implementation guidance for wireless access; and authorizes wireless access to the organization information system prior to allowing such connections that are consistent with the Statewide Standard 8350 System and Communication Protection [NIST 800-53 AC-18].

(P) *Wireless authentication and encryption*: The department shall ensure the organization information system protects wireless access to the organization information system using authentication of users and devices and encryption [NIST 800-53 AC-18(1)] [IRS Pub 1075] [PCI DSS 4.1].

Access control for mobile devices: The department shall establish usage restrictions, configuration/connection requirements, and implementation guidance for department-controlled mobile devices; and authorizes connection of mobile devices to organization information systems [NIST 800-53 AC-19].

(P) *Full device encryption*: The department shall employ full-device encryption to protect the confidentiality and integrity of information on mobile devices authorized to connect to organization information systems or to create, transmit, or process confidential information [NIST 800-53 AC-19(5)] [IRS Pub 1075] [HIPAA 164.308 (e)(2)(ii)—Addressable] [PCI DSS 4.1].

Use of external information systems: The department shall establish terms and conditions, consistent with any trust relationships established with other organizations owning, operating, and/or maintaining external information systems, allowing authorized individuals to access the information system from external information systems; and process, store, or transmit department-controlled information using external information systems [NIST 800-53 AC-20].

(P) *Limits on authorized use*: The department shall permit authorized individuals to use an external information system to access the organization information system to process, store, or transmit department-controlled information only when the department [NIST 800-53 AC-20(1)] [IRS Pub 1075]:
1. Verifies the implementation of required security controls on the external system as specified in the departments' information security policies and security plan, or
2. Retains approved information system connection or processing agreements with the organizational entity hosting the external information system in accordance with the State Library Records Retention Schedule, Management Records

(P) *Portable storage devices*: The department shall restrict or prohibit the use of department-controlled portable storage devices by authorized individuals on external information systems [NIST 800-53 AC-20(2)] [IRS Pub 1075].

(P) *Information sharing*: The department shall facilitate information sharing by enabling authorized users to determine whether access authorizations assigned to the sharing partner match the access restrictions on the information for department-defined circumstances; and shall employ mechanisms or processes to assist users in making information sharing/collaboration decisions [NIST 800-53 AC-21] [IRS Pub 1075] [PCI DSS 12.8].

(P) *Maintain list of service providers*: The department shall maintain a list of service providers that have access to confidential data [PCI DSS 12.8.1].

(P) *Written agreements*: The department shall maintain a written agreement that includes an acknowledgment that the service providers are responsible for the security of confidential data the service providers possess [PCI DSS 12.8.2].

(P) *Due diligence*: The department shall ensure there is an established process for engaging service providers, including proper due diligence prior to engagement [PCI DSS 12.8.3].

(P) *Service provider monitoring program*: The department shall maintain a program to monitor service provider's compliance with requirements for the protection of confidential data [PCI DSS 12.8.4].

Publicly accessible content: The department shall [NIST 800-53 AC-22]

1. Designate individuals authorized to post information onto a publicly accessible information system
2. Train authorized individuals to ensure that publicly accessible information does not contain nonpublic information
3. Review the proposed content of information prior to posting onto the publicly accessible organization information system to ensure that nonpublic information is not included
4. Review the content on the publicly accessible organization information system for nonpublic information annually and removes such information, if discovered

A.3.3 Policy Example: 8330 System Security Audit

Purpose: The purpose of this policy is to protect organization information systems and data by ensuring the department and organization information systems have the appropriate controls and configurations to support audit log generation, protection, and review.

Scope: This policy shall apply to all organization information systems:

- (P)—Policy statements preceded by "(P)" are required for organization information systems categorized as protected.

A.3.3.1 Policy Statements   *Audit events*: The department shall [NIST 800-53 AU-2]

1. Determine that the organization information system is capable of auditing the events listed in the Statewide System Security Audit Standard S8330
2. Coordinate the security audit function with other organizational entities requiring audit-related information to enhance mutual support and to help guide the selection of auditable events
3. Provide a rationale for why the auditable events are deemed to be adequate to support after-the-fact investigations of security incidents
4. Ensure the events listed in the Statewide System Security Audit Standard S8330 are logged within the organization information system

   (P) *Audit reviews and updates*: The department shall review and update the selected audited events annually, or as required [NIST 800-53 AU-2(3)] [IRS Pub 1075]

Content of audit records: The department shall ensure the organization information system generates audit records containing information that establishes [NIST 800-53 AU-3]

1. What type of event occurred [PCI DSS 10.3.2] [IRS Pub 1075]
2. When the event occurred [PCI DSS 10.3.3] [IRS Pub 1075]
3. Where the event occurred [PCI DSS 10.3.5] [IRS Pub 1075]
4. The source of the event (i.e., name of the affected data, system component, or resource) [PCI DSS 103.6] [IRS Pub 1075]
5. The outcome of the event [PCI DSS 10.3.4]

6. The identity of any individuals or subjects associated with the event [PCI DSS 10.3.1] [IRS Pub 1075]

(P) *Additional audit information*: The department shall ensure the state information system generates audit records containing department-defined additional information. [NIST 800-53 AU-3(1)] [IRS Pub 1075]

Audit storage capacity: The department shall allocate audit record storage capacity in accordance with department-defined audit record storage requirements [NIST 800-53 AU-4].

Response to audit processing failures: The department shall ensure the organization information system alerts department-defined personnel or roles in the event of an audit processing failure; and shuts down the organization information system, overwrites the oldest audit records, or stops generating audit records [NIST 800-53 AU-5].

Audit review, analysis, and reporting: The department shall review and analyze organization information system audit records periodically for indications of inappropriate or unusual activity; and reports findings to department-defined personnel or roles. Department information systems with CHD shall perform this review daily [NIST 800-53 AU-6] [HIPAA 164.308 (a)(1)(ii)(D)] [HIPAA 164.312 (b)] [PCI DSS 10.6].

(P) *Process integration*: The department shall employ automated mechanisms to integrate audit review, analysis, and reporting processes to support organizational processes for investigation and response to suspicious activities [NIST 800-53 AU-6(1)] [IRS Pub 1075].

(P) *Correlate audit repositories:* The department shall analyze and correlate audit records across different repositories to gain department-wide situational awareness [NIST 800-53 AU-6(3)] [IRS Pub 1075].

Audit reduction and report generation: The department shall ensure the organization information system provides an audit reduction and report generation capability that supports on-demand audit review, analysis, and reporting requirements and after-the-fact investigations of security incidents; and does not alter original audit records [NIST 800-53 AU-7].

(P) *Automatic processing*: The department shall ensure the organization information system provides the capability to process audit records for events of interest based on the following audit fields within audit records [NIST 800-53 AU-7(1)] [IRS Pub 1075]:

1. Individual identities
2. Event types
3. Event locations
4. Event times and time frames
5. Event dates
6. System resources involved and Internet Protocol (IP) addresses involved
7. Information object accessed

Time stamps: The department shall ensure the organization information system uses internal system clocks to generate time stamps for audit records; and generates time in the time stamps that can be mapped to Coordinated Universal Time or Greenwich Mean Time and provides a granularity of time to a department-defined unit of time [NIST 800-53 AU-8].

(P) *Synchronization with authoritative time source*: The department shall ensure the organization information system synchronizes internal organization information system clocks a department-defined frequency with a department-defined time source when the time difference is greater than a department-defined time period [NIST 800-53 AU-8(1)] [IRS Pub 1075] [PCI DSS 10.4.1, 10.4.3].

(P) *Protection of time data*: The department shall ensure the organization information system protects time-synchronization settings by restricting access to such settings to authorized personnel and logging, monitoring, and reviewing changes [PCI DSS 10.4.2].

Protection of audit information: The department shall ensure the organization information system protects audit information and audit tools from unauthorized access, modification, and deletion [NIST 800-53 AU-9] [PCI DSS 10.5] [IRS Pub 1075].

(P) *Access by subset of privileged users*: The department shall authorize access and modification to management of audit functionality to only a department-defined subset of privileged users [NIST 800-53 AU-9(4)] [IRS Pub 1075] [PCI DSS 10.5.1, 10.5.2].

(P) *Audit trail backup*: The department shall promptly back up audit trail files to a centralized log server or media that is difficult to alter [PCI DSS 10.5.3].

(P) *Audit backup on separate physical systems*: The department shall ensure the organization information system backs up audit records onto a physically different system or system component than the system or component being audited [PCI DSS 10.5.4].

(P) *File integrity monitoring of audit logs*: The department shall ensure the organization information system uses file integrity monitoring or change detection software on audit logs to ensure that existing log data cannot be changed without generating alerts. New audit data being added to audit logs do not cause such alerts [PCI DSS 10.5.5].

Audit record retention: The department shall retain audit records for a department-defined time period with a department-defined time period available for immediate analysis to provide support for after-the-fact investigations of security incidents and to meet regulatory and organizational information retention requirements. For organization information systems with CHD, these defined times are at least 1 year with a minimum of 3 months immediately available for analysis [NIST 800-53 AU-11] [PCI DSS 10.7]. However, all state departments must comply with Arizona State Library, Archives and Public Records rules and implement, whichever retention period is most rigorous, binding, or exacting.

Audit generation: The department shall ensure the organization information system [NIST 800-53 AU-12]

1. Provides audit record generation capability for the auditable events at servers, firewalls, workstations, and other department-defined system components
2. (P) Antivirus programs are generating audit logs [PCI DSS 5.2]

3. Allows department-defined personnel or roles to select which auditable events are to be audited by specific components of the organization information system
4. Generates audit records for the events with the content defined in Section 0 (Content of Audit Records)

A.3.4 Policy Example: 8340 Identification and Authentication

Purpose: The purpose of this policy is to define the security requirements for establishing and maintaining user accounts for organization information systems.

Scope: This policy shall apply to all organization information systems:

- (P)—Policy statements preceded by "(P)" are required for organization information systems categorized as protected.

A.3.4.1 Policy Statements   *Identification and authentication of organizational users:* The department shall ensure the organization information system uniquely identifies and authenticates organizational users (or processes acting on behalf of organizational users) [NIST 800 53 IA-2] [PCI DSS 8.1] [HIPAA 164.312 (a)(2)(i), (d)].

Network access to privileged accounts: The department shall ensure the organization information system implements multifactor authentication for network access to privileged accounts [NIST 800 53 IA-2(1)].

(P) *Network access to nonprivileged accounts*: The department shall ensure the organization information system implements multifactor authentication for nonprivileged accounts [NIST 800 53 IA-2(2)] [IRS Pub 1075].

(P) *Local access to privileged accounts*: The department shall ensure the organization information system implements multifactor authentication for local access to privileged accounts [NIST 800 53 IA-2(3)] [IRS Pub 1075].

(P) *Network access to privileged accounts—replay resistant*: The department shall ensure the organization information system implements replay-resistant authentication mechanisms for network access to privileged accounts [NIST 800 53 IA-2(8)] [IRS Pub 1075].

(P) *Remote access to privileged accounts—separate device*: The department shall ensure the organization information system implements multifactor authentication for remote access to privileged accounts such that one of the factors is provided by a device separate from the system gaining access and the device meets statewide cryptographic standards for strength of mechanism [NIST 800 53 IA-2(11)] [PCI DSS 8.3] [IRS Pub 1075].

(P) *Remote access to nonprivileged accounts—separate device*: The department shall ensure the organization information system implements multifactor authentication for remote access to nonprivileged accounts such that one of the factors is provided by a device separate from the system gaining access and the device meets statewide cryptographic standards for strength of mechanism [NIST 800 53 IA-2(12)] [IRS Pub 1075] [PCI DSS 8.3].

(P) *Device identification and authentication*: The department shall ensure the organization information system uniquely identifies and authenticates before establishing a local, remote, or network connection [NIST 800 53 IA-3] [IRS Pub 1075] [PCI DSS 8.1] [HIPAA 164.312 (d)].

Identifier management: The department shall manage the organization information system identifiers by [NIST 800 53 IA-4] [PCI DSS 8.5, 8.5.1]

1. (P) Ensuring that group, shared, or generic account identifiers and authentication methods are not used [PCI DSS 8.5.8]
2. Receiving authorization from department-defined personnel or roles to assign individual, role, or device identifier
3. Selecting an identifier that identifies an individual, role, or device
4. Assigning the identifier to the intended individual, role, or device
5. Preventing reuse of identifiers for 1 year
6. Disabling the identifier after 90 days of inactivity [PCI DSS 8.5.5]

Authenticator management: The department shall manage the organization information system authenticators (e.g., passwords, tokens, certificate, and key cards) by [NIST 800 53 IA-5] [HIPAA 164.308(a)(5)ii)(D)] [HIPAA 164.308 (d)]

1. Verifying, as part of the initial authenticator distribution, the identity of the individual, group, role, or device receiving the authenticator [PCI DSS 8.5.2]
2. Establishing initial authenticator content for authenticators defined by the department (e.g., password policy)
3. Ensuring that authenticators have sufficient strength of mechanism for their intended use
4. Establishing and implementing administrative procedures for initial authenticator distribution, for lost/compromised or damaged authenticators, and for revoking authenticators
5. Changing default content of authenticators prior to organization information system installation
6. Establishing minimum and maximum lifetime restrictions and reuse conditions for authenticators
7. Changing/refreshing authenticators (department-defined time period by authenticator type [e.g., passwords, tokens, biometrics, public key infrastructure (PKI) certificates, and key cards])
8. Protecting authenticator content from unauthorized disclosure and modification
9. Requiring individuals to take, and having devices implement, specific security safeguards to protect authenticators
10. Changing authenticators for role accounts when membership to those accounts changes
11. Employing at least one of the following methods to authenticate all users [PCI DSS 8.1]:
    a. Password-based authentication
    b. PKI-based authentication
    c. In person or trusted third-party registration
    d. Hardware token-based authentication

Password-based authentication: The department shall ensure the organization information system, for password-based authentication enforces password controls consistent with the

Statewide Standard 8340, Identification and Authentication [NIST 800 53 IA-5(1)].

(P) *PKI-based authentication:* The department shall ensure the organization information system, for PKI-based authentication [NIST 800 53 IA-5(2)] [IRS Pub 1075]:

1. Validates certifications by constructing and verifying a certification path to an accepted trust anchor, including checking certificate status information
2. Enforces authorized access to the corresponding private key
3. Maps the authenticated identity to the account of the individual or group
4. Implements a local cache of revocation data to support path discovery and validation in case of inability to access revocation information using the network

(P) *In person or trusted third-party registration:* The department shall require that the registration process to receive authenticators be conducted in person or by a trusted third party before the registration authority with authorization by department-defined personnel or roles [NIST 800 53 IA-5(3)] [IRS Pub 1075].

Hardware token-based authentication: The department shall ensure the organization information system, for hardware token-based authentication, employs mechanisms that satisfy department-defined token quality requirements (e.g., compliant with a particular PKI) [NIST 800 53 IA-5(11)].

Authenticator feedback: The department shall ensure the organization information system obscures feedback of authentication information during the authentication process to protect the information from possible exploitation/use by unauthorized individuals [NIST 800 53 IA-6].

Cryptographic module authentication: The department shall ensure the organization information system implements mechanisms for authentication to a cryptographic module that meets the requirements of applicable federal laws, state laws, executive orders, directives, policies, regulations, standards, and guidance for such authentication [NIST 800 53 IA-7].

Identification and authentication (nonorganizational users): The department shall ensure the organization information system uniquely identifies and authenticates nonorganizational users (or processes acting on behalf of nonorganizational users) [NIST 800 53 IA-8] [PCI DSS 8.1] [HIPAA 164.312 (a)(2)(i), (d)].

> *Acceptance of third-party credentials*: The department shall ensure the organization information system accepts Federal Identity, Credential, and Access Management (FICAM)-approved third-party credentials [NIST 800 53 IA-8(2)].
>
> *Use of FICAM-approved products*: The department shall employ only FICAM-approved organization information system components in organization information systems to accept third-party credentials [NIST 800 53 IA-8(3)].
>
> *Use of FICAM-issued profiles*: The department shall ensure the organization information system conforms to FICAM-issued implementation profiles [NIST 800 53 IA-8(4)].

A.3.5 Policy Example: 8350 System and Communication Protections

Purpose: The purpose of this policy is to establish the baseline controls for the protection of organization information systems and their communications.

Scope: This policy shall apply to all organization information systems:

- (P)—Policy statements preceded by "(P)" are required for organization information systems categorized as protected.
- (P-PCI)—Policy statements preceded by "(P-PCI)" are required for organization information systems with PCI data (e.g., CHD).
- (P-FTI)—Policy statements preceded by "(P-FTI)" are required for organization information systems with federal taxpayer information.

A.3.5.1 Policy Statements Network and architectural controls: The department shall ensure the organization information system implements the following network and network architectural controls:

> (P) *Application partitioning*: The department shall ensure the organization information system separates user functionality

(including user interface services) either physically or logically from organization information system management functionality (e.g., privileged access) [NIST 800 53 SC-2] [IRS Pub 1075].

Boundary protection: The department shall ensure the organization information system [NIST 800 53 SC-7]

1. Monitors and controls communications at the external boundary of the system and at key internal boundaries within the system

2. Implements subnetworks for publicly accessible system components that are logically separated from internal organizational networks

3. Connects to external networks of information systems only through managed interfaces consisting of boundary protection devices arranged in accordance with organizational security architecture

    (P) *Implement demilitarized zone (DMZ)*: The department shall ensure the organization information system prohibits direct public access between the Internet and any system component in the protected organization information system. The DMZ [PCI DSS 1.3]

    1. Limits inbound traffic to only system components that provide authorized publicly accessible services, protocols, and ports [PCI DSS 1.3.1]

    2. Limits inbound Internet traffic to IP addresses within the DMZ [PCI DSS 1.3.2]

    3. Does not allow any direct connections inbound or outbound for traffic between the Internet and the protected organization information system [PCI DSS 1.3.3]

    4. Does not allow internal addresses to pass from the Internet into the DMZ [PCI DSS 1.3.4]

    5. Does not allow unauthorized outbound traffic from the protected organization information system to the Internet [PCI DSS 1.3.5]

    6. Implements stateful inspection, also known as dynamic packet filtering (i.e., only established connections are allowed into the network) [PCI DSS 1.3.6]

7. Places system components that store confidential data (such as a database) in an internal network zone, segregated from the DMZ and other untrusted networks [PCI DSS 1.3.7]

8. Does not disclose private IP addresses and routing information to unauthorized parties (Note: methods to obscure IP addressing may include network address translations, placing servers behind proxy servers, removal route advertisements for private networks that employ registered addressing, or internal use of request for comment (RFC) 1918 address space instead of registered addresses) [PCI DSS 1.3.8]

(P) *Firewall configuration*: The department shall build firewall and router configurations that restrict access points between nonprotected systems (standard organization information systems or untrusted networks) and any system components in the protected organization information system. The configurations [PCI DSS 1.2]

1. Restrict inbound and outbound traffic to that which is necessary for the protected organization information system [PCI DSS 1.2.1]

2. Secure and synchronize router configuration files [PCI DSS 1.2.2]

3. Implement perimeter firewalls between any wireless networks and the Protected organization information system, and these firewalls are configured to deny or control (if such traffic is necessary for business purposes) any traffic from the wireless environment into the protected organization information system [PCI DSS 1.2.3]

(P) *Limit access points*: The department shall limit the number of external network connections to the organization information system [NIST 800 53 SC-7(3)] [IRS Pub 1075].

(P) *Deny by default/allow by exception*: The department shall ensure the organization information system at managed interfaces denies network communications traffic by default and allows network communications traffic by exception (i.e., deny all, permit by exception) [NIST 800 53 SC-7(5)] [IRS Pub 1075].

(P) *Network disconnect*: The department shall ensure organization information system terminates the network connections associated with a communications session at the end of the session or after 15 min of inactivity [NIST 800 53 SC-10] [IRS Pub 1075].

Server controls: The department shall ensure the organization information system implements the following controls for servers and components of the organization information system:

(P) *Information in shared resources*: The department shall ensure the organization information system prevents unauthorized and unintended information transfer using shared system resources [NIST 800 53 SC-4] [IRS Pub 1075].

(P) *Prevent split tunneling for remote devices*: The department shall ensure the organization information system, in conjunction with a remote device, prevents the device from simultaneously establishing nonremote connections with the system and communicating using some other connection to resources in external networks [NIST 800 53 SC-7(7)] [IRS Pub 1075].

(P) *Single primary function (database)*: The department shall ensure organization information system components (e.g., servers) implementing a database implement only one primary function (the database) on this server [PCI DSS 2.2.1].

(P-PCI) *Single primary function*: For organization information systems storing, processing, or transmitting CHD, the department shall ensure all organization information system components (e.g., server) implement only one primary function per server to prevent functions that require different security levels from coexisting on the same server [PCI DSS 2.2.1].

(P) *Minimum and secure services*: The department shall ensure the organization information system component (e.g., server) enables only necessary and secure services, protocols, daemons, etc. as required for the function of the system.

1. (P-PCI) PCI: For organization information systems with CHD unnecessary functionality such as scripts, drivers,

features, subsystems, file systems, and unnecessary web servers must be removed [PCI DSS 2.2.2, 2.2.4].

2. (P) *Otherwise protected*: For all other organization information systems unnecessary functionality such as scripts, drivers, features, subsystems, file systems, and unnecessary web servers must be disabled or removed [PCI DSS 2.2.2, 2.2.4].

(P) *Secure configuration*: The department shall configure the organization information system component (e.g., server) security parameters to prevent misuse [PCI DSS 2.2.3].

Secure services: The department shall ensure the organization information system implements the following controls for services provided:

Denial of service protection: The department shall ensure the organization information system protects against or limits the effects of the following types of denial of service attacks, defined in Standard 8350, System and Communication Protection, by employing boundary protection devices with packet filtering capabilities and, if required by the department, employing increased capacity and bandwidth combined with service redundancy [NIST 800 53 SC-5].

(P) *Cryptographic services*: The department shall ensure the organization information system implements the following cryptographic services:

1. (P) *Cryptographic protection*: The organization information system shall implement Federal Information Processing Standards validated cryptography for the protection of confidential information during transmission over open public networks and in accordance with applicable federal and state laws, executive orders, directives, policies, regulations, and standards [NIST 800 53 SC-13] [PCI DSS 4.1] [HIPAA 164.312(a)(2)(iv), (e)(2)(i)].

2. (P) *Cryptographic key establishment and management*: The department shall establish and manage cryptographic keys for required cryptography employed within the organization information system in accordance with statewide requirements for key generation, distribution, storage, access, and destruction [NIST 800 53 SC-12].

(P) *Key protection*: The department shall protect all keys used to secure confidential data against disclosure and misuse [PCI DSS 3.5]:

1. Restrict access to cryptographic keys to the fewest number of custodians necessary [PCI DSS 3.5.1]
2. Store cryptographic keys securely in the fewest possible locations and forms [PCI DSS 3.5.2]

(P) *Key management process*: The department shall fully document and implement all key-management processes and procedures for cryptographic keys used for encryption of confidential data including the following [PCI DSS 3.6]:

1. Generation of strong cryptographic keys [PCI DSS 3.6.1]
2. Secure cryptographic key distribution [PCI DSS 3.6.2]
3. Secure cryptographic key storage [PCI DSS 3.6.3]
4. Cryptographic key changes for keys that have reached the end of their crypto-period, as defined by the associated application vendor or key owner, and based on industry best practices and guidelines [PCI DSS 3.6.4]
5. Retirement or replacement of keys as deemed necessary when the integrity of the key has been weakened, or keys are suspected of being compromised [PCI DSS 3.6.5]
6. If manual clear-text cryptographic key-management operations are used, these operations must be managed using split knowledge and dual control [PCI DSS 3.6.6]
7. Prevention of unauthorized substitution of cryptographic keys [PCI DSS 3.6.7]
8. Requirement for cryptographic key custodians to formally acknowledge that they understand and accept their key-custodian responsibilities [PCI DSS 3.6.8]

(P) *Public key infrastructure certificates*: The department shall obtain public key certificates from an approved service provider [NIST 800 53 SC-17] [IRS Pub 1075].

(P) *External telecommunications services*: The department shall ensure [NIST 800 53 SC-7(4)] [IRS Pub 1075]
1. Implement a managed interface for each external telecommunication service
2. Establish a traffic flow policy for each managed interface
3. Protect the confidentiality and integrity of the information being transmitted across each interface
4. Document each exception to the traffic flow policy with a supporting mission/business need and duration of that need
5. Review exceptions to the traffic flow policy annually and removes exceptions that are no longer supported by an explicit mission/business need

(P) *Transmission confidentiality and integrity*: The department shall ensure the organization information system protects the confidentiality and, if required, integrity of transmitted information [NIST 800 53 SC-8] [IRS Pub 1075] [HIPAA 164.312(c)(1), (c)(2), (e)(1)].
(P) *Cryptographic or alternate physical protection*: The department shall ensure the organization information system prevents unauthorized disclosure of information and, if required, detects changes to information during transmission [NIST 800 53 SC-8(1)] [IRS Pub 1075] [HIPAA 164.312(c)(1), (c)(2), (e)(1)].

(P) *Mobile code*: The department shall [NIST 800 53 SC-18] [IRS Pub 1075]
1. Define acceptable and unacceptable mobile code and mobile code technologies (e.g., Java, JavaScript, ActiveX, Postscript, PDF, Shockwave movies, Flash animations, and VBScript)
2. Establish usage restrictions and implementation guidance for acceptable mobile code and mobile code technologies
3. Authorize, monitor, and control the use of mobile code within the organization information system

Collaborative computing devices: The department shall ensure the organization information system prohibits remote activation of collaborative computing devices with the following exceptions: cameras and microphones in support of remote conferences and training; and provides an explicit indication of use to users physically present at the devices [NIST 800 53 SC-15].

(P) *Voice over Internet protocol (VoIP)*: The department shall establish usage restrictions and implementation guidance for VoIP technologies based on the potential to cause damage to the information system if used maliciously; and authorizes, monitors, and controls the use of VoIP within the prospective area [NIST 800 53 SC-19] [IRS Pub 1075].

(P) *Session authenticity*: The department shall ensure the organization information system protects the authenticity of communication sessions. Note: This control addresses communications protections at the session, versus packet level and establishes grounds for confidence at both ends of communications sessions in ongoing identities of other parties and in the validity of information transmitted. Authenticity protection includes, for example, protecting against man-in-the-middle attacks/session hijacking and the insertion of false information into sessions [NIST 800 53 SC-23] [IRS Pub 1075].

Secure name/address resolution service: The department shall ensure the organization information system implements the following with respect to secure name/address resolution service:

1. *Secure name/address resolution service (authoritative service)*: The department shall ensure the organization information system provides additional data origin and integrity artifacts along with the authoritative name resolution data the system returns in response to external name/address resolution queries; and provides the means to indicate the security status of child zones and (if the child supports secure resolution services) to enable verification of a chain of trust among parent and child domains, when operating as part of a distributed, hierarchical namespace [NIST 800 53 SC-20].

2. *Secure name/address resolution service (recursive or caching resolver)*: The department shall ensure the organization information system requests and performs data origin authentication and data integrity verification on the name/address resolution responses the system receives from authoritative sources [NIST 800 53 SC-21].

3. *Architecture and provisioning for name/address resolution service*: The department shall ensure the organization information systems that collectively provide name/address resolution service for an organization are fault-tolerant and implement internal/external role separation [NIST 800 53 SC-22].

(P) *Protection of information at rest*: The department shall ensure the organization information system protects the integrity of audit log data at rest [NIST 800 53 SC-28].

(P-FTI) *Protection of taxpayer information at rest*: For systems with taxpayer information, the department shall ensure the organization information system protects the confidentiality and integrity of taxpayer information at rest [IRS Pub 1075].

A.4 Information Privacy Policy Example

Based on the Arizona Policy and Standards project, one policy was created to address the operations of the information security program.

A.4.1 Policy Example: 8410 System Privacy

Purpose: The purpose of this standard is to provide more detailed guidance for the development of a system privacy notice based on standards, regulations, and best practices.

Scope: This policy shall apply to all organization information systems:

- (P)—Policy statements preceded by "(P)" are required for organization information systems categorized as protected.

A.4.1.1 Policy Statements *Authority to collect*: The department shall determine and document the legal authority that permits the

collection, use, maintenance, and sharing of PII, either generally or in support of a specific program or organization information system need. For additional specificity on the authority to collect, refer to Standard 8330, System Security Audit [NIST 800 53 AP-1] [Privacy Acts] [HIPAA 164.520(a)(1)].

Purpose specification: The department shall describe the purpose(s) for which PII is collected, used, maintained, and shared in its privacy notices [NIST 800 53 AP-2] [HIPAA 164.520(a)(1)] [ARS 41-4152].

Access enforcement: The department shall ensure the organization information system enforces approved authorizations for logical access to PII in accordance with applicable control policies (e.g., identity-based policies and role-based policies) [NIST 800-53 AC-3].

(P) *Least privilege*: The department shall employ the concept of least privilege, allowing only authorized accesses to PII for users (and processes acting on behalf of users), which are necessary to accomplish assigned tasks in accordance with organizational missions and business functions [NIST 800-53 AC-6].

Governance and privacy program: The department shall [NIST 800 53 AR-1]

1. Appoint a senior department official for privacy accountable for developing, implementing, and maintaining an organization-wide governance and privacy program to ensure compliance with all applicable laws and regulations regarding the collection, use, maintenance, sharing, and disposal of PII by programs and organization information systems [HIPAA 164.530(a)(1)] [EO 2008-10]
2. Monitor federal and state privacy laws for changes that affect the privacy program
3. Allocate resources to implement and operate the organization-wide privacy program
4. Develop a strategic organizational privacy plan for implementing applicable privacy controls, policies, and procedures
5. Develop, disseminates, and implements operational privacy policies and procedures that govern the appropriate privacy and security controls for program, organization information systems, or technologies involving PII
6. Update privacy plan, policies, and procedures annually

Privacy impact and risk assessment: The department shall [NIST 800 53 AR-2]

1. Document and implement a privacy risk management process that assesses privacy risk to individuals resulting from the collection, sharing, storing, transmitting, use, and disposal of PII.
2. Conduct privacy impact assessments (PIAs) for organization information systems, programs, or other activities that pose a privacy risk in accordance with applicable law, policy, or any existing department policies and procedures.
3. Ensure PIAs are conducted prior to any new collection of PII or upon significant changes in the architecture, information flow, or use of PII within existing systems.

Privacy requirements for contractors and service providers: The department shall [NIST 800 53 AR-3]

1. Establish privacy roles, responsibilities, and access requirements for contractors and service providers
2. Include privacy requirements in contracts and other acquisition-related documents

Privacy monitoring and auditing: The department shall monitor and audit privacy controls and internal privacy policy annually to ensure effective implementations [NIST 800 53 AR-4].

Privacy awareness and training: The department shall [NIST 800 53 AR-5]

1. Develop, implement, and update a comprehensive training and awareness strategy aimed at ensuring that organization employees and contractors understand privacy responsibilities and procedures
2. Administer basic privacy training annually and targeted, role-based privacy training for organization employees and contractors having responsibility for PII or for activities that involve PII annually
3. Ensure that organization employees and contractors certify (manually or electronically) acceptance of responsibilities for privacy requirements annually

Privacy reporting: The department shall conduct an initial evaluation, develop, disseminate, and establish and follow a schedule for regularly updating as necessary, but at least every 3 years, reports to the SPO and other appropriate oversight bodies to demonstrate accountability with specific statutory and regulatory privacy program mandates, and to senior management and other personnel with responsibility for monitoring privacy program progress and compliance [NIST 800 53 AR-6].

Privacy-enhanced system design and development: The department shall design organization information systems to support privacy by automating privacy controls [NIST 800 53 AR-7].

Accounting of disclosures: The department, consistent with state privacy acts and subject to any applicable exceptions or exemptions, shall [NIST 800 53 AR-8] [HIPAA 164.528(a)]

1. Keep an accurate accounting of disclosures of information held in each system of records under its control, including
   a. Date, nature, and purpose of each disclosure of a record
   b. Name and address of the person or organization to which the disclosure was made
2. Retain the accounting of disclosures for the life of the record or 5 years after the disclosure is made, whichever is longer or as required by law. However, all state departments must comply with Arizona State Library, Archives and Public Records rules and implement, whichever retention period is most rigorous, binding, or exacting.

Data quality: The department shall [NIST 800 53 DL-1]

1. Confirm to the greatest extent possible upon collection or creation of PII, the accuracy, relevance, timeliness, and completeness of that information
2. Collect PII directly from the individual to the greatest extent practicable
3. Check for, and corrects as necessary, any inaccurate or outdated PII used by its programs or systems annually
4. Issue guidelines ensuring and maximizing the quality, utility, objectivity, and integrity of disseminated information

Data integrity: The department shall [NIST 800 53 DI-2]

1. Document processes to ensure the integrity of PII through existing security controls

Minimization of PII: The department shall [NIST 800 53 DM-1]

1. Identify the minimum PII elements that are relevant and necessary to accomplish the legally authorized purpose of collection
2. Limit the collections and retention of PII to the minimum elements identified for the purposes described in the notice and for which the individual has provided consent
3. Conduct an initial evaluation of PII holdings, and establishes and follows a schedule for regularly reviewing those holdings at least every 3 years and update as necessary to ensure that only PII identified in the notice is collected and retained, and that the PII continues to be necessary to accomplish the legally authorized purpose

Data retention and disposal: The department shall [NIST 800 53 DM-2]

1. Retain each collection of PII for department-defined time period to fulfill the purposes identified in the notice or as required by law
2. Dispose of, destroy, erases, and/or anonymize the PII, regardless of the method of storage, in accordance with an Arizona State Library-approved record retention schedules and in a manner that prevents loss, theft, misuse, or unauthorized access [ARS 44-7601] [ARS 41-151.12]
3. Use techniques, documented in the Policy 8250, Media Protection, to ensure secure deletion or destruction of PII (including originals, copies, and archived records)

Consent: For collection, use, and disclosures of PII not already authorized by law, the department shall [NIST 800 53 IP-1]

1. Provide means, where feasible and appropriate, for individuals to authorize the collection, use, maintaining, and sharing of PII prior to its collection [HIPAA 164.522(a)(1)]

2. Provide appropriate means for individuals to understand the consequences of decisions to approve or decline the authorization of the collection, use, dissemination, and retention of PII

3. Obtain consent, where feasible and appropriate, from individuals prior to any new uses or disclosure of previously collected PII

4. Ensure that individuals are aware of and, where feasible, consent to all uses of PII not initially described in the public notice that was in effect at the time the organization collected the PII

Individual access: The department, consistent with the laws and regulations, and subject to any applicable exceptions or exemptions, shall [NIST 800 53 IP-2] [HIPAA 164.524(a)]

1. Provide individuals the ability to have access to their PII maintained in its system(s) of records

2. Publish rules and regulations governing how individuals may request access to records maintained in a system of records [HIPAA 164.524(b),(c),(d)]

3. Adhere to requirements and policies and guidance for the proper processing of PII requests

Redress: For collection, use, and disclosures of PII not already authorized by law, the department shall [NIST 800 53 IP-3] [HIPAA 164.526(a)–(f)]

1. Provide a process for individuals to have inaccurate PII maintained by the organization corrected or amended, as appropriate

2. Establish a process for disseminating corrections or amendments of the PII to other authorized users of the PII, such as external information sharing partners and, where feasible and appropriate, notifies affected individuals

Complaint management: For collection, use, and disclosures of PII not already authorized by law, the department shall implement a process for receiving and responding to complaints, concerns, or questions from individuals about the department privacy practices [NIST 800 53 IP-4] [HIPAA 164.530(d)].

Inventory of PII: The department privacy officer shall [NIST 800 53 SE-1]

1. Establish, maintain, and update at least every 3 years an inventory that contains a listing of all programs and department information systems identified as collecting, using, maintaining, or sharing PII
2. Provide each update of the PII use to the department CIO or department ISO at least every 3 years to support the establishment of information security requirements for all new or modified department information systems containing PII

Privacy incident response: The department shall [NIST 800 53 SE-2]

1. Develop and implement a privacy incident response plan consistent with requirements in Statewide Policy Framework 8240 Incident Response Planning
2. Provide an organized and effective response to privacy incidents in accordance with the department privacy incident response plan

Privacy notice: The following guidance is offered for the development of a privacy notice: [NIST 800 53 TR-1] [HIPAA 164.520(c)] [ARS 41-4152]

1. Provides effective notice to the public and to individuals regarding
   a. Its activities that impact privacy, including its collection, use, sharing, safeguarding, maintenance, and disposal of PII
   b. Authority for collection PII
   c. The choices, if any, individuals may have regarding how the department uses PII and the consequences of exercising or not exercising those choices
   d. The ability to access and have PII amended or corrected, if necessary
   e. Describes the following:
      i. How the department collects the PII and the purpose(s) for which it collects that information
      ii. How the department uses PII internally
      iii. Whether the department shares PII with external entities, the categories of those entities, and the purposes for such sharing

     iv. Whether individuals have the ability to consent to specific uses of sharing of PII and how to exercise any such consent

     v. How individuals may obtain access to PII

     vi. How the PII will be protected

  f. Revises its public notices to reflect changes in practice or policy that affect PII or changes in its activities that impact privacy, before or as soon as practicable after the change

  g. Provides notice in clear and conspicuous language when individuals are first asked to provide PII to the department

Dissemination of privacy program information: The department shall [NIST 800 53 TR-3]

1. Ensure the public has access to information about its privacy notice and is able to communicate with its privacy officer
2. Ensure that its privacy notice are publicly available through department websites or public-facing email addresses and/or phone lines that enable the public to provide feedback and/or direct questions to privacy offices regarding privacy notice

Internal use: The department shall use PII internally only as authorized by law or for the authorized purpose(s) described in privacy notice [NIST 800 53 UL-1].

Information sharing with third parties: The department shall [NIST 800 53 UL-2] [HIPAA 164.508(a)]

1. Share PII externally, only as authorized by law or for the authorized purposes identified and described in privacy notice or in a manner compatible with those purposes
2. Where appropriate, enter into memoranda of understanding, memoranda of agreement, letters of intent, computer matching agreements, SLAs, business associate agreements, or similar agreements, with third parties that specifically describe the PII covered and specifically enumerate the purposes for which the PII may be used and offers the same level of protection as documented in this policy [HIPAA 164.514(e)(4)]

3. Monitor, audit, and train its staff on the authorized sharing of PII with third parties and on the consequences of unauthorized use of sharing of PII
4. Evaluate any proposed new instances of sharing PII with third parties to assess whether the sharing is authorized and whether additional or new privacy notice is required

Appendix B: Example Departmental Policy Tailoring Guide

This guide was developed to assist those assisting departments in the tailoring of information security policy templates into departmental information security policies. The guide provides general guidance for all departments and, where appropriate, specific guidance for "small departments" versus "large departments."

B.1 Suggested Discussion with Department

Individual departments may have a myriad of questions or concerns regarding the information security policy tailoring project. However, they may not know where to begin in discussing the project. The discussion outline provided in Table B.1 has been useful in discussions with other departments and is documented as a suggested discussion agenda.

B.2 Addressing "Department-Defined" and "Department-Specified" Requirements

Within the policy, standard, and procedures (PSP) templates, there are 34 occurrences of a placeholder in the requirement for the department to define or specify an element of the requirement. These placeholders

Table B.1   Department PSP Project Meeting Discussion Template

TOPIC	INSTRUCTIONS	DISCUSSION
Systems discussion	Talk to the department about the number and type of systems they have	*Single system*. Smaller departments will benefit from calling all of their system components (e.g., servers, laptops, and web apps) a single system. This greatly simplifies the process.
		User of other's systems. Departments that are given a login to another organization's or another company's system may typically consider that system to be owned by the other organization or company. Examples include e-banking, application service providers (e.g., salesforce.com), and systems run by other departments in fulfillment of the other organization's mission.
Sensitive data discussion	Talk to the department about any sensitive data they may have	If the department's system contains any confidential data, then all requirements (standard system requirements and protected system requirements) indicated with a (P) apply. Many departments will simply know that they have sensitive data and that can end the discussion, but for those departments that are not sure, ask specifically about the following types of data that may be on their systems.
		Medical records. Many licensing boards in the medical profession have these records.
		Cardholder data (CHD). If the department has a merchant ID, then they need to comply with PCI Data Security Standard (DSS). If they do not know if they have a merchant ID, they should check with their finance person. *Note*. Many departments have their credit card processing run through an organization system in which the organization retains the merchant ID (and has a sub-ID for each department). If this is the department's only credit card processing, then they do not need to comply with PCI DSS and they may not have CHD in their system.
		Other. Ask the department what other information their system stores, transmits, or processes that may be considered confidential.

(*Continued*)

Table B.1 (*Continued*) Department PSP Project Meeting Discussion Template

TOPIC	INSTRUCTIONS	DISCUSSION
The PSP tailoring project	If the department has any question regarding the project, discuss them here	*Due dates.* The draft policies are due from each department by July 1. If the department has any exceptions to the PSP template, then they will indicate the exception. With each exception, the department shall indicate the requirement number and the requested change. If the requested change is a strengthening of the requirement, nothing else is required. If the requested change is not, then the department shall include a description of compensating controls or a risk-based rationale of why the change makes sense.
		Outsourced and external services. Many departments ask why they need to create policies if they outsource all the administration of the systems to someone else (e.g., information technology). Let them know that the department is responsible for the protection of their data. If they choose to outsource these functions, they need to ensure that the entity they outsource it to is required to protect the data. The policies do not need to be modified depending on who administers the systems. You may point them to the following.
		P8130 System acquisition policy.
		When outsourcing, contracts must include security requirements.
		The department must implement a service-level agreement and provide oversight of this agreement.
Writing the policies	To write the department's policies, the following steps are required	Globally replace "department" in each document with the name of the organization.
		Define/specify parameters and/or values for each requirement with the phrase "department-defined" or "department-specified." There are 34 such instances. This guide provides a reference and a discussion for each of these instances in Table B.2.
		Confirm adoption of each requirement OR request a policy exception. This is done in Section 4 of each policy and must have either (a) a list of compensating controls or (b) a risk rationale for each requested policy exception.

Note: When meeting with each department, the topics of the discussion are likely to cover systems, data confidentiality, the PSP tailoring project, and the approach to writing policies.

Table B.2 Department-Defined and Department-Specified Placeholders in the PSP Templates

POLICY	POLICY TITLE	TITLE	REQUIREMENT TEXT	DEPARTMENT-DEFINED DISCUSSION	DEFAULT "EASY" REQUIREMENT
8120	Information security program	Security risk assessment	Disseminate risk assessment results to the department CIO, department ISO, organization information system owner, and other *department-defined* personnel or roles	Define the roles within the department that should receive this report. Larger departments may include an auditing function, a compliance officer, a librarian, or other roles that require a copy of this report. Smaller departments may collapse the number of roles receiving this report to include the CIO and executive director only	Disseminate risk assessment results to the organization director and designated information technology (IT) manager
		Vulnerability scanning	Share information obtained from the vulnerability scanning process and security control assessments with *department-defined* personnel or roles to help eliminate similar vulnerabilities in other organization information systems (i.e., systemic weaknesses or deficiencies)	Define the roles within the department that should receive this report. Larger departments may include multiple roles within the IT departments and security departments, or other roles that require a copy of this information. Smaller departments may collapse the number of roles receiving this information to include the CIO and executive director only	Share information obtained from the vulnerability scanning process and security control assessments with organization director and designated IT manager to help eliminate similar vulnerabilities in other organization information systems (i.e., systemic weaknesses or deficiencies)
		Vulnerability scanning: Provide privileged access	The organization information system implements privileged access authorization to *department-defined* components containing highly confidential data (e.g., databases)	Define components within the department information system that contain highly confidential data. This will include databases for most departments with confidential data but other components such as cloud storage, check processing systems, or vital records systems may be listed as well. These systems	The organization information system implements privileged access authorization to databases

(Continued)

Table B.2 (*Continued*)   Department-Defined and Department-Specified Placeholders in the PSP Templates

POLICY	POLICY TITLE	TITLE	REQUIREMENT TEXT	DEPARTMENT-DEFINED DISCUSSION	DEFAULT "EASY" REQUIREMENT
				should be listed if privileged access vulnerability scanning is judged to be an essential control for these components risk-based decision	
		Continuous monitoring	Ongoing security status monitoring of *department-defined* metrics in accordance with the department's continuous monitoring strategy	Define metrics to be collected and monitored to implement your department's security program. Departments should look to information technology, internal audit, information security or other departments security program as an example of useful security metrics	The organization monitors the security status of the organization information system by recording and reporting to the organization director on a quarterly basis the following security program metrics:
				Percentage taken SAT in last 12 months	Percentage of organization employees and contractors that have taken security awareness training in the last 12 months
				Aging of temporary accounts	Aging of temporary accounts
				Number of security incidents detected (H,M,L)	Number of security incidents detected prioritized by high, moderate, and low risk
				Date of last: RA, VS, PT, ARR, policy update, and SSP update	Date of last: risk assessment, vulnerability scan, penetration test, account rights review, policy update, and system security plan update

(Continued)

Table B.2 (*Continued*)　Department-Defined and Department-Specified Placeholders in the PSP Templates

POLICY	POLICY TITLE	TITLE	REQUIREMENT TEXT	DEPARTMENT-DEFINED DISCUSSION	DEFAULT "EASY" REQUIREMENT
8130	System security acquisition	Technology life cycle	Manage the organization information system using a *department-defined* technology life cycle that incorporates information security considerations	Define your department's technology life cycle. Include a listing and definition of its stages in your supporting documentation	The organization technology life cycle includes the following phases: Requirements Acquisition Deployment Disposition Information security considerations are incorporated into each of these phases to ensure security compliance and protection of sensitive data
		State information system documentation	Ensure documentation is available to *department-defined* personnel or roles	Define the roles within the department that should receive this information. Larger departments may include multiple roles within the IT departments and security departments, or other roles that require a copy of this information. Smaller departments may collapse the number of roles receiving this information to include the CIO and executive director only	Ensure documentation is available to privileged users and administrators

(Continued)

Table B.2 (*Continued*) Department-Defined and Department-Specified Placeholders in the PSP Templates

POLICY	POLICY TITLE	TITLE	REQUIREMENT TEXT	DEPARTMENT-DEFINED DISCUSSION	DEFAULT "EASY" REQUIREMENT
8220	System security maintenance	Information system monitoring	Identify unauthorized use of the organization information system through *department-defined* intrusion-monitoring tools	List the intrusion-monitoring tools your department utilizes	In order to identify unauthorized use of the organization information system, the organization monitors logs from the following intrusion-monitoring tools: Antivirus Firewalls [Web content filtering] [Intrusion detection system]
8250	Media protection	Media use	The department shall restrict the use of [*department-specified* type of digital media] on [*department-specified* organization information systems and/or system components]	List any media restricted by your department. If this list changes according to certain components (e.g., no USB thumb drives in laptops), then specify which type of digital media is restricted for each component. Many departments may not list any restrictions; in which case this requirement may simply state, "The department does not restrict the use of any types of digital media on department organization information systems"	The organization has no restrictions on the use of digital media on organization information systems or system components

(*Continued*)

Table B.2 (*Continued*) Department-Defined and Department-Specified Placeholders in the PSP Templates

POLICY	POLICY TITLE	TITLE	REQUIREMENT TEXT	DEPARTMENT-DEFINED DISCUSSION	DEFAULT "EASY" REQUIREMENT
8280	Acceptable use	User-based technology agreements	The user-based technology access agreements shall be developed by the department and contains *department-defined* security controls. Standard 8220, system security maintenance provides guidance to departments for minimum recommended user-based technology controls	Define specific security controls for any user-based technology used within your department (e.g., iPads and smart phones). Many departments may not allow any user-based technology. Others may not have any restrictions on it. At a minimum, the department should review the standard S8220 for minimum recommended controls	The user-based technology access agreements (e.g., smart phones) shall be developed by the organization and contains the following security controls: PIN authentication Encrypted transmission Encrypted storage Report when lost Remote wipe
8310	Account management	Separation of duties (SoD)	The department shall separate *department-defined* duties, document SoD of individuals, and define organization information system access authorizations to support SoD	SoD is a security control to be employed when a single person should not be involved from beginning to end on a single task or when looking to establish oversight and governance. Departments should establish their own SoD requirements. Some of the areas to look into these requirements include sensitive transactions such as accounts payable/accounts receivable, new code moving to production, security controls implementation, and design and audit. Departments that outsource account management and/or administration should consider enforcing a separation between	The organization has no SoD requirements within the organization information system

(Continued)

Table B.2 (*Continued*) Department-Defined and Department-Specified Placeholders in the PSP Templates

POLICY	POLICY TITLE	TITLE	REQUIREMENT TEXT	DEPARTMENT-DEFINED DISCUSSION	DEFAULT "EASY" REQUIREMENT
		Automated audit actions	The department shall ensure the organization information system automatically audits account creation, modification, enabling, disabling, and removal actions and notifies, as required *department-defined* personnel or roles	privileged account holders and those who review audit logs of these commands Define the roles within the department that should receive this report. Larger departments may include an auditing function, a compliance officer, a librarian, or other roles that require a copy of this report. Smaller departments may collapse the number of roles receiving this report to include the CIO and executive director only	The organization shall ensure the organization information system automatically audits account creation, modification, enabling, disabling, and removal actions and notifies the organization director and designated IT manager
		Automatic removal of temporary accounts	The organization information system automatically removes or disables temporary and emergency accounts after a *department-defined* time	Define number of days that may pass before a temporary or emergency account should be disabled. Emergency accounts should be short lived (e.g., 1–7 days) and temporary accounts may be longer term (e.g., 7–90 days)	The organization information system automatically removes or disables temporary and emergency accounts after 7 days and temporary accounts after 30 days
		Disable inactive accounts	The department shall ensure the organization information system automatically disables inactive accounts after *department-defined* time period. For organization information systems containing CHD, the time period must be no less than 90 days	Define number of days that may pass before an inactive account should be disabled. PCI requires that this be no more than 90 days	The organization shall ensure the organization information system automatically disables inactive accounts after 90 days

(Continued)

Table B.2 (*Continued*)   Department-Defined and Department-Specified Placeholders in the PSP Templates

POLICY	POLICY TITLE	TITLE	REQUIREMENT TEXT	DEPARTMENT-DEFINED DISCUSSION	DEFAULT "EASY" REQUIREMENT
8320	Access control	Information flow enforcement	The department shall ensure the organization information system enforces approved authorizations for controlling the flow of information within the system and between interconnected systems based on *department-defined* information flow control policies, including policy 8350, systems and communications protection. These policies prohibit direct public access between the Internet and any system component in the protected organization information system	Define the information flows allowed by your department's firewalls. The design principle of the firewall ("Default Deny All") means that only department-required flows (e.g., external request to port 80) shall be allowed by the firewall	The organization shall ensure the organization information system enforces approved authorizations for controlling the flow of information within the system and between interconnected systems based on the *Department Firewall Rules Document*
		Unsuccessful logon attempts	The department shall ensure the organization information system enforces a department-specified limit of consecutive invalid logon attempts by a user; and automatically locks the account/node for a *department-specified* period of time or locks the account/node until released by an administrator when the maximum	Define the period of time that an account shall be locked when too many password guesses have been attempted. Any amount of time over 15 min will address most threats to password guessing but departments may want to set this period to several hours or 1 day	The organization shall ensure the organization information system enforces a limit of five consecutive invalid logon attempts by a user; and automatically locks the account/node for a 15 min or locks the account/node until released by an administrator when the maximum number of unsuccessful attempts is exceeded *(Continued)*

Table B.2 (*Continued*) Department-Defined and Department-Specified Placeholders in the PSP Templates

POLICY	POLICY TITLE	TITLE	REQUIREMENT TEXT	DEPARTMENT-DEFINED DISCUSSION	DEFAULT "EASY" REQUIREMENT
			number of unsuccessful attempts is exceeded, consistent with the Access Control Standard 8320		
		System use notification	Displays to users a *department-defined* notification banner before granting access to the system that provides privacy and security notices consistent with applicable federal laws, state laws, executive orders, directives, policies, regulations, standards, and guidance	Define the department notification banner to be used in the web facing applications and systems and the (potentially different) use notification for internal systems Templates for such a notification may be available. Also, the system use notification may have been established before and already in use. Departments should carefully review the banner to which information security and technology leads as well as the privacy and legal officers to ensure it is appropriate and accurate	Displays to users a notification banner before granting access to the system that provides privacy and security notices consistent with applicable federal laws, state laws, executive orders, directives, policies, regulations, standards, and guidance

(Continued)

Table B.2 (*Continued*) Department-Defined and Department-Specified Placeholders in the PSP Templates

POLICY	POLICY TITLE	TITLE	REQUIREMENT TEXT	DEPARTMENT-DEFINED DISCUSSION	DEFAULT "EASY" REQUIREMENT
		Session lock	The department shall ensure the organization information system prevents further access to the system by initiating a *department-specified* limit of time inactivity or upon receiving a request from a user; and retains the session lock for a *department-specified* limit of time or until the user reestablishes access using established identification and authentication procedures. If the user does not reestablish access within a *department-specified* limit of time, the session is dropped	Define the period of inactivity that requires a session to be locked. Consider 5–15 min Define the period of time the session shall be locked. It is suggested that there is no period of time for the session lock and instead the session is locked until the user reestablishes access Define the period of inactivity that requires a session to be dropped. Consider 30–60 min	The organization shall ensure the organization information system prevents further access to the system by initiating a time limit of 15 min of inactivity or upon receiving a request from a user; and retains the session lock for until the user reestablishes access using established identification and authentication procedures. If the user does not reestablish access within a 1 h, the session is dropped

(*Continued*)

Table B.2 (*Continued*) Department-Defined and Department-Specified Placeholders in the PSP Templates

POLICY	POLICY TITLE	TITLE	REQUIREMENT TEXT	DEPARTMENT-DEFINED DISCUSSION	DEFAULT "EASY" REQUIREMENT
		Privileged access commands	The department shall authorize the execution of privileged commands and access to security-relevant information using remote access only for *department-defined* needs, and documents the rationale for such access in the security plan for the organization information system	In general, privileged commands (e.g., changing firewall rules and establishing a user account) should be done onsite and not exposed to remote access. However, the department may have a business need to have certain privileged commands executed over a remote session for business reasons despite the risk. In these cases, the department should document these privileged commands, the circumstances in which it would be allowed and a rationale for such access. This is to be documented in the system security plan	The organization restricts the execution of privileged commands and access to security-relevant information using remote access
		Information sharing	The department shall facilitate information sharing by enabling authorized users to determine whether access authorizations assigned to the sharing partner match the access restrictions on the information for *department-defined* circumstances; and shall employ mechanisms or processes to assist users in making information sharing/collaboration decisions	If the department determines a business need for information sharing with a partner, then the circumstances in which it shares information and any restrictions on that access (e.g., time of day, type of file, transmission methods, and encryption requirements) shall be documented in this requirement	The organization does not allow information sharing to any sharing partners

(*Continued*)

Table B.2 (Continued) Department-Defined and Department-Specified Placeholders in the PSP Templates

POLICY	POLICY TITLE	TITLE	REQUIREMENT TEXT	DEPARTMENT-DEFINED DISCUSSION	DEFAULT "EASY" REQUIREMENT
8330	System security audit	Audit storage capacity	The department shall allocate audit record storage capacity in accordance with *department-defined* audit record storage requirements	Define the amount of storage space to be allocated for audit. This may be specified in many ways but it is best specified by number of days of audit records	The organization shall allocate audit record storage capacity for 90 days of audit record storage
		Response to audit processing failures	The department shall ensure the organization information system alerts *department-defined* personnel or roles in the event of an audit processing failure; and shuts down the organization information system, overwrites the oldest audit records, or stops generating audit records	Define the roles within the department that should receive this report. Larger departments may include multiple roles within IT that require this information. Smaller departments may simply indicate a single IT role	The organization shall ensure the organization information system alerts the organization director and designated IT manager in the event of an audit processing failure; and shuts down the organization information system, overwrites the oldest audit records, or stops generating audit records
		Audit review, analysis, and reporting	The department shall review and analyze organization information system audit records periodically for indications of inappropriate or unusual activity; and reports findings to *department-defined* personnel or roles. State information systems with CHD shall perform this review daily	Define the roles within the department that should receive this report. Larger departments may include an auditing function, a compliance officer, a librarian, or other roles that require a copy of this report. Smaller departments may collapse the number of roles receiving this report to include the CIO and executive director only	The organization shall review and analyze organization information system audit records periodically for indications of inappropriate or unusual activity, and reports findings to department, the organization director, and designated IT manager. Department information systems with CHD shall perform this review daily

(Continued)

Table B.2 (Continued)   Department-Defined and Department-Specified Placeholders in the PSP Templates

POLICY	POLICY TITLE	TITLE	REQUIREMENT TEXT	DEPARTMENT-DEFINED DISCUSSION	DEFAULT "EASY" REQUIREMENT
		Time stamps	The department shall ensure the organization information system uses internal system clocks to generate time stamps for audit records, and generates time in the time stamps that can be mapped to Coordinated Universal Time (UTC) or Greenwich Mean Time (GMT) and provides a granularity of time to a *department-defined unit of time*	Define the granularity of time to be provided in time stamps for audit records. In general, a granularity of 1 s would be adequate to support most investigations. If the department has a need for a higher level of granularity, then it should be noted here	The organization shall ensure the organization information system uses internal system clocks to generate time stamps for audit records, and generates time in the time stamps that can be mapped to UTC or GMT and provides a granularity of time to 1 s
		Synchronization with authoritative time source	The department shall ensure the organization information system synchronizes internal organization information system clocks to a *department-defined frequency* with a *department-defined* time source when the time difference is greater than a *department-defined* time period	Define frequency by which system clocks are synchronized. In general, once an hour would suffice Define time source in which to synchronize with (National Institute of Standards and Technology provides an Internet time service but others may suffice as well) Define time period by which system clocks would be determined to be out of synch. In general, a 1 s misalignment should be corrected	The organization shall ensure the organization information system synchronizes internal organization information system clocks hourly with an organization-approved time source when the time difference is greater than 1 s

(Continued)

Table B.2 (*Continued*) Department-Defined and Department-Specified Placeholders in the PSP Templates

POLICY	POLICY TITLE	TITLE	REQUIREMENT TEXT	DEPARTMENT-DEFINED DISCUSSION	DEFAULT "EASY" REQUIREMENT
		Access by subset of privileged users	The department shall authorize access and modification to management of audit functionality to only a *department-defined* subset of privileged users	Define role of privileged users who have the authority to modify system audit (e.g., monitoring and logging) functions, parameters, and files. It is a design principle to ensure that this include a subset of all privileged users to ensure oversight of this privileged function	The organization shall authorize access and modification to management of audit functionality only to organization IT administrators
		Audit record retention	The department shall retain audit records for a *department-defined* time period with a *department-defined* time period available for immediate analysis to provide support for after-the-fact investigations of security incidents and to meet regulatory and organizational information retention requirements. For organization information systems with CHD, these defined times are at least 1 year with a minimum of 3 months immediately available for analysis	Define amount of time audit records shall be retained. Include time frame for immediate analysis (i.e., stored online) and time frame available in long term storage. Unless there is a burden to storing these records, it is recommended that you follow the 3 months/1 year guidance required for systems with CHD, even if you do not have such data	The department shall retain audit records for a 1 year with 3 months available for immediate analysis to provide support for after-the-fact investigations of security incidents and to meet regulatory and organizational information retention requirements

(Continued)

Table B.2 (*Continued*) Department-Defined and Department-Specified Placeholders in the PSP Templates

POLICY	POLICY TITLE	TITLE	REQUIREMENT TEXT	DEPARTMENT-DEFINED DISCUSSION	DEFAULT "EASY" REQUIREMENT
			The department shall ensure the organization information system provides audit record generation capability for the auditable events, defined in Section 6.1 (audit records), at servers, firewalls, workstations, and other *department-defined* system components	List any system components, besides servers, firewalls, and workstations that may produce useful audit records. At a minimum include laptops	The organization shall ensure the organization information system provides audit record generation capability for the auditable events, defined in Section 6.1 (audit records), at servers, firewalls, workstations, laptops, and databases
			The department allows *department-defined* personnel or roles to select which auditable events are to be audited by specific components of the organization information system	Define role that has the system privilege to select which events are audited	The department allows organization IT administrators to select, which auditable events are to be audited by specific components of the organization information system
8340	Identification and authentication	Identifier management	The department shall manage the organization information system identifiers by receiving authorization from *department-defined* personnel or roles to assign individual, role, or device identifier	Define role that authorizes the assignment of a system identifier (e.g., user ID) to an individual. This may be the supervisor or human resources	The organization shall manage the organization information system identifiers by receiving authorization from the organization director, human resources, or designated IT staff

(*Continued*)

Table B.2 (Continued) Department-Defined and Department-Specified Placeholders in the PSP Templates

POLICY	POLICY TITLE	TITLE	REQUIREMENT TEXT	DEPARTMENT-DEFINED DISCUSSION	DEFAULT "EASY" REQUIREMENT
		Authenticator management	The department shall manage the organization information system authenticators (e.g., passwords, tokens, certificate, and key cards) by changing/refreshing authenticators [*department-defined* time period by authenticator type (e.g., passwords, tokens, biometrics, public key infrastructure (PKI) certificates, and key cards)]	Define the time period in which authenticators shall be refreshed. It is suggested that passwords be changed every 90 days and tokens (both hard and soft tokens) be refreshed every 1–2 years based on manufacturer recommendations (e.g., battery life, key management, and software upgrades)	The organization shall refresh passwords every 90 days, tokens every 2 years, certificates every 2 years, and key cards every 4 years
		In person or trusted third-party registration	The department shall require that the registration process to receive authenticators be conducted in person or by a trusted third party before the registration authority with authorization by *department-defined* personnel or roles	Define role that authorizes the assignment of a system identifier (e.g., user ID) to an individual. This may be the supervisor or human resources	The organization shall require that the registration process to receive authenticators be conducted in person with authorization by the organization director, human resources, or designated IT staff
		Hardware token-based authentication	The department shall ensure the organization information system, for hardware token-based authentication, employs mechanisms that satisfy *department-defined* token quality requirements (e.g., compliant with a particular PKI)	Define the PKI with which a token must comply (e.g., organizational PKI and department PKI)	The organization shall ensure the organization information system uses only organization-approved hardware token devices

(Continued)

Table B.2 (*Continued*) Department-Defined and Department-Specified Placeholders in the PSP Templates

POLICY	POLICY TITLE	TITLE	REQUIREMENT TEXT	DEPARTMENT-DEFINED DISCUSSION	DEFAULT "EASY" REQUIREMENT
8350	System and communication protection	Transmission confidentiality and integrity	Cryptographic or alternate physical protection—the department shall ensure the organization information system prevents unauthorized disclosure of information and, if required, detects changes to information during transmission unless otherwise protected by *department-defined* alternative physical safeguards	Either protect transmissions technically (i.e., encryption) or through alternative physical means. Examples of physical protection include pressurized conduit or protected distribution systems. If you choose technical means only delete the text beginning with "unless"	The organization shall ensure the organization information system prevents unauthorized disclosure of information and detects changes to information during transmission
8410	System privacy	Data retention and disposal	The department shall retain each collection of personally-identifiable information (PII) for *department-defined* time period to fulfill the purposes identified in the notice or as required by law, refer to policy DRAFT, document retention	Define time period for retention of PII. This needs to be consistent with laws and the state librarian guidance. The Arizona State Library has an online application that covers retention schedules on an organization-by-organization basis	The organization shall retain each collection of PII for the time period necessary to fulfill the purposes identified in the notice and in compliance with the following schedules: [List department retention schedules as listed on the organizational]

Note: Each department is instructed to replace these placeholders with a department-defined or department-specified value or statement.

are there because the requirement does not lend itself to a strict definition or assignment that may fit all departments. The flexibility of
the placeholders allows each department to tailor the policy to meet
their specific need.

This is likely to be an area of PSP tailoring that either gets over-
looked (i.e., the department simply leaves the requirements as-is,
resulting in an incomplete requirement) or is the source of confusion
for some departments. It would be useful to engage the department
in a discussion to point out these placeholders and let the department know that they must be defined and specified. If the department needs assistance in determining the value of parameters or the
creation of statements for the placeholders, Table B.2 provides some
guidance. Table B.2 provides an index to the requirements within the
PSP templates where a department will need to define or specify an
element of the requirement to tailor it to the department's needs.

FREQUENTLY ASKED QUESTIONS

Q1: We are a small organization and risk assessments cost a lot of
money. Can we perform "annual" risk assessments every other
year?

A1: You may request a policy exception on this requirement. Include
either compensating controls (e.g., we run vulnerability scans
every month) or provide a risk rationale (e.g., our system is a
standard system in a static environment).

While you are at it, you should consider your policy requirements for

- Vulnerability scanning (required quarterly and when new
vulnerabilities are identified for all systems standard and
protected)
- Wireless access point (AP) testing (required quarterly for
all systems standard and protected)
- Penetration testing (required annually for protected
systems)

Q2: Do we need to have a distinct line item for security in our
budget? Budgets are set by the legislature and they come back as
a lump sum.

A2: The requirement states that the line item for security must be in the "organizational programming and budgeting documentation." This is our own department's documents and not from the legislature that is required.

Q3: I am a small organization; what am I going to spend on security?

A3: Common elements of a security budget include the cost of the following: antimalware subscriptions, anticipated expenditures on security components (e.g., firewalls and intrusion detection system [IDS]), cost of risk assessment, penetration test, vulnerability scans, wireless scanning, anticipated incident handling, security awareness training, and security technical training and conferences.

Q4: The requirement for marking media states that we have to mark digital and nondigital media. Our department sends out a lot of papers and it would be onerous for us to label it all. Do we really have to do that?

A4: If you truly believe it is in the best interest of the citizen and your organization to send out paper copies (or digital media) of sensitive information without labeling them, you could request an exception but this seems a rather high risk. Consider some methods that may make it easier to comply such as stock paper with a labeled header and footer for high-volume hard-copy productions, binding materials together and labeling the front cover, and obtaining digital media drives with labels printed on them.

Q5: Visitor badges: The requirement for physical protection states that we must give the visitor a badge or sticker for access to our facility. We are a small organization, all working in a single room, and a badge seems overkill.

A5: This may be a good requirement for a risk-based exception. If you consider the risk of a visitor being onsite without a clear indication that he or she is a visitor, then request an exception here. Your compensating controls are (a) all areas of the office are viewable by multiple staff members, (b) all employees are well known to each other, and (c) visitors are all escorted and supervised.

Q6: Visitor log: Do we really need a visitor log? We do not get many visitors. This seems to be a hassle.

A6: A visitor log is a rather easy control to implement. It consists of a log book with columns for the name, organization, date, and times. It is suggested that the visitor log also include a signature block for the visitor to indicate that they agree to the "on premise" acceptable use policy. Include a laminated copy of this policy as part of the book.

Q7: Fire suppression: The requirement is for fire suppression and detection devices for the system. Does this include our office space?

A7: The requirement is intended to cover anywhere a system component resides, including the office space. The requirement is for any type of fire suppression and detection, so sprinkler systems and smoke detectors count. If you are housed in a facility without any such protection (first ensure your building is compliant with code), request for an exception on those facilities that have no such systems and list compensating controls such as handheld fire extinguishers.

Q8: Temperature and humidity monitoring: Am I required to monitor the temperature of my office environment because it houses workstations?

A8: No. The requirement is for data centers, computer rooms, and server rooms.

Q9: [All] Requirement references: We do not need to comply with Health Insurance Portability and Accountability Act or Payment Card Industry (PCI), so I removed those requirements. Is that OK?

A9: Not exactly. You may request an exception to any other requirements based on perceived risk or compensating controls. The references at the end of each requirement (shown in square brackets) refer to the source of the requirement. This is not intended as an applicability indicator. The indication at the beginning of the requirement (e.g., (P), (P-PHI)) denotes applicability.

Index